I0223462

Peter Königs
Problems for Moral Debunkers

Peter Königs

Problems for Moral Debunkers

——

On the Logic and Limits of Empirically Informed Ethics

DE GRUYTER

ISBN 978-3-11-135845-1
e-ISBN (PDF) 978-3-11-075019-5
e-ISBN (EPUB) 978-3-11-075021-8

Library of Congress Control Number: 2021950456

Bibliographic information published by the Deutsche Nationalbibliothek
The Deutsche Nationalbibliothek lists this publication in the Deutsche Nationalbibliografie;
detailed bibliographic data are available on the internet at http://dnb.dnb.de.

© 2023 Walter de Gruyter GmbH, Berlin/Boston
This volume is text- and page-identical with the hardback published in 2022.

Cover image: akinbostanci / iStock / Getty Images Plus
Printing and binding: CPI books GmbH, Leck

www.degruyter.com

Acknowledgments

This book is a substantially revised and expanded version of my doctoral thesis, which was submitted to the Faculty of Philosophy of Tübingen University in 2018. I would like to thank my supervisor, Sabine Döring, for her guidance, advice, and support during my work on this book and in the years before. It was also Sabine who, teaching a seminar on metaethics when I was an undergraduate at Tübingen University, sparked my interest in analytic philosophy in the first place, for which I am grateful to this day. My work has benefited greatly from countless inspiring discussions in her *Oberseminar*.

I am very grateful for the thorough and insightful comments on the manuscript provided by Sabine and my other two examiners, Thomas Grundmann and Klaus Corcilius. I would also like to thank Richard Holton, who welcomed me as a visiting student in Cambridge and commented extensively on my work.

For helpful conversations about some of the themes of this book and for comments on parts of the manuscript, I would also like to thank Alex Wiegmann, Anika Lutz, Bahadir Eker, Carel van Schaich, Chiara Brozzo, Christian Seidel, Christoph Lumer, Emilian Mihailov, Eva-Maria Düringer, Folke Tersman, Gregor Hochstetter, Hanno Sauer, Herman Philipse, Hong-Yu Wong, Irina Schumski, Jean Moritz Müller, Joachim Horvath, Katharina Brecht, Krisztina Orbán, Leo Hoeft, Leo Menges, Malte Hendrickx, Michael Wenzler, Moritz Hildt, Nicholas Meinzer, Nora Heinzelmann, Norbert Paulo, Paulina Sliwa, Raymond Geuss, Ruth Rebecca Tietjen, Thomas Sattig, Wolfgang M. Schröder as well as audiences in Bochum, Cologne, Karlsruhe, Osnabrück, Porto, Saarbrücken, Tübingen and Utrecht. Uschi Wiedmaier patiently provided expert administrative help.

I am indebted to the *Studienstiftung des deutschen Volkes*, which generously funded my graduate studies and my research stay in Cambridge.

I am deeply thankful to my friends, who have been a great source of encouragement. My special thanks go to my family – my father Ludger, my mother Karin and my brother Sebastian – for their invaluable moral support. My greatest gratitude is due to my wife Katharina, whose love and companionship were the greatest inspiration in the past years.

I would also like to thank *Springer* and *Taylor & Francis* for granting me permission to revise and reuse previously published material. In Chapters 3 and 4, I have drawn on, and in part significantly revised and expanded, material from "Experimental Ethics, Intuitions, and Morally Irrelevant Factors" (*Philosophical Studies*, *177*(9), 2020) and "On the normative insignificance of neuroscience and dual-process theory" (*Neuroethics*, *11*(2), 2018). Chapter 5 includes my "Two Types of Debunking Arguments" (*Philosophical Psychology*, *31*(3), 2018). Chapter 7

https://doi.org/10.1515/9783110750195-001

is based on "Evolutionary Skepticism about Morality and Prudential Normativity" (*Philosophia*, 46(4), 2018).

Contents

1 Introduction

1.1 Debunking arguments

Debunking arguments are arguments of the form "you just believe that because...".[1] They challenge a belief by showing this belief to have a questionable genealogy. Consider the following thought experiment: Imagine there is a pill that makes you believe that Napoleon lost Waterloo. Now imagine

> that you are proceeding through life happily believing that Napoleon lost Waterloo (as, indeed, you are), and then you discover that at some point in your past someone slipped you a 'Napoleon lost Waterloo' belief pill. [...] [Y]ou somehow discover beyond any shred of doubt that your belief is the product of such a pill. Should this undermine your faith in your belief that Napoleon lost Waterloo? Of course it should.[2]

This intuitively compelling thought experiment, due to Richard Joyce, conveys a good idea of what debunking arguments are. Roughly, the strategy is that of showing that the targeted belief has its causal source in a belief-forming process that fails to track the truth. And awareness of the fact that one's belief originates from a non-truth-tracking process should prompt one to abandon this belief. It renders continuing having this belief epistemically unjustified.

Debunking arguments occupy an ambivalent position in philosophy. On the one hand, the idea of discrediting a doctrine – moral or otherwise – by looking at its genealogy has a rich philosophical history. The heyday of genealogical debunking arguments was the late 19th and early 20th century, which witnessed three of the most influential genealogical debunkers in the history of philosophy: Sigmund Freud, Karl Marx and Friedrich Nietzsche.[3] In *The Future of an Illusion*, Freud demasks people's belief in God as, precisely, an illusion that has its origins in an unconscious wish for a strong father-figure.[4] Marx's theory of ideology has it that a society's dominant religious and political views are just vehicles of the interests of the ruling class: "Law, morality, religion are to [the proletarian] so many bourgeois prejudices, behind which lurk in ambush just as many bourgeois interests."[5] And Nietzsche, in his *Genealogy of Morals*, debunks ascetic moralities, such as Christian morality, as resentment-driven attempts to come

---

1 White, 2010.
2 Joyce, 2006, p. 179.
3 I am here following Leiter, 2004.
4 Freud, 1961.
5 Marx and Engels, 2012, p. 48.

https://doi.org/10.1515/9783110750195-002

to terms with the meaninglessness of suffering.[6] What unites these three authors is their commitment to a naturalistic methodology and the notion that understanding the origins of beliefs can render them epistemically suspect.[7] This methodological insight can be traced back much further to the early days of philosophy. Early instances of debunking arguments, which bear a striking resemblance to some of the above, can be found in the Platonic dialogues. In Plato's *Politeia*, Thrasymachus notoriously claims that justice is what serves the interests of the powerful, a claim that may be interpreted as a sociological debunking explanation of popular conceptions of justice. In quite a Marxian fashion, he contends that the norms of justice are put in place by the rulers to manipulate the weak in an attempt to promote the formers' interests.[8] And in *Gorgias*, Callicles, anticipating Nietzsche, holds the opposing view that the moral norms have been determined by the weak in an effort to keep down the more gifted and capable: "[T]o prevent these men from having more than themselves they say that taking more is shameful and unjust, and that doing injustice is this, seeking to have more than other people."[9]

On the other hand, it is a common-place, especially among analytic philosophers, that the genesis of a belief and its truth or validity are two entirely different things that must not be conflated. Since it is the philosopher's task to determine the latter, genealogical considerations do not belong in philosophical argumentation. A *locus classicus* for this assumption is Hans Reichenbach's *Experience and Prediction*. He introduces the terms 'context of discovery' and 'context of justification' and maintains "that epistemology is only occupied in constructing the context of justification."[10] Not only has it typically been assumed that genealogical aspects can be bracketed when we engage in philosophy with an epistemic intent.[11] Often, the much stronger claim is made that genealogical reasoning is fallacious. Genealogical arguments are routinely dismissed as genetic fallacies. Philosophers in the analytic tradition especially pride themselves with assessing the merits of a theory exclusively by assessing the evidence for and against it, rather than by looking at how it originated or who its authors are. The following statement by John Searle is worth quoting at length as it en-

---

6 Nietzsche, 1996.
7 See again Leiter, 2004.
8 Plato, 2012, 338e–339a; see Barney, 2011; Höffe, 2013, p. 75.
9 Plato, 1979, 483c; see Höffe, 2013, p. 75.
10 Reichenbach, 1938, pp. 6–7.
11 Of course, historians of philosophy have a legitimate interest in the genealogy of ideas for its own sake.

capsulates how analytic philosophers tend to think about genealogical arguments:

> A standard argumentative strategy of those who reject the Western Rationalistic Tradition is to challenge some claim they find objectionable, by challenging the maker of the claim in question. Thus, the claim and its maker are said to be racist, sexist, phono-phallo-logocentric, and so forth. To those who hold the traditional conception of rationality, these challenges do not impress. They are, at best, beside the point. To those within the Western Rationalistic Tradition, these types of challenge have names. They are commonly called argumentum ad hominem and the genetic fallacy. Argumentum ad hominem is an argument against the person who presents a view rather than against the view itself, and the genetic fallacy is the fallacy of supposing that because a theory or claim has a reprehensible origin, the theory or claim itself is discredited. I hope it is obvious why anyone who accepts the idea of objective truth and therefore of objective knowledge thinks this is a fallacy.[12]

The strategy of debunking a philosophical doctrine by discrediting its genesis is informed by the assumption that this strict distinction between genesis and validity, as suggested by Searle and many others, is untenable.

Although the idea that the genealogy of a belief might tell us something about its truth is not new, recent years have seen a renaissance of philosophical interest in debunking explanations. In moral philosophy in particular, debunking explanations have become a popular, if controversial, argumentative device.

One debunking project, carried out by Joshua Greene and Peter Singer, invokes genealogical findings in an attempt to debunk deontological moral theory and vindicate utilitarianism. Deontological intuitions are exposed as mere remnants of natural selection, as sensitive to morally irrelevant factors, and as dysfunctional. More sophisticated defenses of deontology, which do not rest on the debunked intuitions, are dismissed as mere products of confabulatory post hoc rationalization.[13]

A more far-reaching evolutionary debunking argument has been advanced by Sharon Street, who takes evolutionary forces to have messed with virtually all our evaluative dispositions. As a result, there is little reason to assume that our evaluative beliefs are even anywhere near the evaluative truth. This, at least, follows if we operate within a realist framework, which posits a Platonic realm of evaluative truths that are independent of our evaluative attitudes. If we adopt a constructivist, attitude-dependent framework, the fact that our beliefs have been influenced by evolutionary processes should not lead us to

---

12 Searle, 1993, p. 66.
13 See in particular Greene, 2008, 2014; Singer, 2005.

doubt their correctness. In light of the implausibility of radical evaluative skepticism, Street suggests that we reject realism and embrace constructivism.[14]

A third debunking project focuses on the evolution of our moral sense as such, rather than on evolution's impact on the contents of our moral beliefs. Richard Joyce has suggested that our very tendency to think in moral categories and to judge actions in moral terms is explainable in evolutionary terms. And like Greene, Singer and Street, Joyce takes it that a naturalistic evolutionary explanation along these lines has an undermining effect on the justification of our beliefs. He concludes that our belief in the existence of moral facts is unjustified.[15]

This book assesses the merits and prospects of debunking arguments in moral philosophy. It proceeds by exploring these three routes of debunking widely shared moral commitments. Before I say more about the aim and structure of this book, however, I wish to take the opportunity to provide a more panoramic overview of the many potential uses and varieties of genealogical critique to convey an impression of the diversity and versatility of debunking arguments. Debunking arguments can differ in a wide range of aspects, among which are their subject matter, scope, ambition, level of defeat, reason for defeat, dialectical function and direction.[16]

1.2 Varieties of debunking arguments

Subject matter

The present study deals with debunking arguments in moral philosophy. It should be kept in mind, though, that the applicability of the debunking method is by no means limited to beliefs related to morality. Beliefs about any subject matter are, in principle, amenable to debunking explanations. While debunking arguments in moral philosophy have arguably been at the center of attention in the current debate surrounding debunking arguments, there are noteworthy examples of debunking arguments in other fields and disciplines.[17]

Traditionally, debunking arguments have been particularly popular in political theory. Karl Marx, one of the most influential debunkers in political theory,

---

14 See in particular Street, 2006, 2016.
15 See in particular Joyce, 2006.
16 For a different typology, see Sauer, 2018, ch. 3.
17 I am here only considering debunking arguments in different fields of philosophy. Debunking arguments have been applied outside of philosophy, too, but they will not be reviewed here.

has already been mentioned. Marx' critique of ideology and his notion that the superstructure of society – its culture, belief system, political institutions, etc. – are determined by a society's economic arrangements has been very influential among left-leaning political theorists. Indeed, it has inspired an entire research program aimed at understanding and demasking ideology.[18] While critique of ideology is typically associated with the left, debunking explanations have also been employed by libertarians in an effort to make sense of why libertarianism has garnered so little support both within and outside the academy. In his *Why do Intellectuals Oppose Capitalism?*, Robert Nozick attempts to explain why intellectuals of the 'wordsmith' type – journalists, authors, literary critics, etc. – tend to be on the left of the political spectrum and to resent capitalist society.[19] He suspects that their resentment is due to differences in how two important social institutions, the school and the market, distribute praise and rewards. At school, the wordsmith's skills are the most highly valued ones. This instills in those who later go on to become authors or journalists a feeling of superiority and entitlement. In a free market, by contrast, the skills of the wordsmith are worth relatively little. The capitalist society denies verbally gifted people the status of superiority that they have grown to feel entitled to. Their rejection of capitalism is a response to this humiliation. This speculative suggestion is not entirely without irony, given that Marxist Louis Althusser, in his classic *Ideology and Ideological State Apparatuses*, has identified the educational system as the institution that is chiefly responsible for perpetuating capitalist ideology.[20] More recently, Michael Huemer has devoted a chapter of his book-length defense of anarcho-capitalism to exploring the biases that might account for the near-unanimous but, in his view, misguided belief in the legitimacy and authority of the state.[21]

Another popular target for debunking explanations, which we briefly encountered above, are religious beliefs. Again, the idea of explaining away religious belief has a long history that can be traced back far beyond the likes of Freud and Nietzsche.[22] But as in the field of moral philosophy, advancements in the empirical sciences – especially in evolutionary biology and the cognitive sciences – have generated renewed interest in the natural mechanisms underlying religious belief and in the possibility of demystifying religion as an entirely

---

18 For an overview, Eagleton, 1991.
19 Nozick, 1997.
20 Althusser, 1971.
21 Huemer, 2013, pp. 101–136. For another notable attempt to debunk opposition to laissez-faire capitalism, see von Mises, 1972.
22 For a historical overview, refer to Mason, 2010, pp. 771–773.

natural phenomenon. Protagonists of a research program called 'the cognitive science of religion' include David Sloan Wilson and Daniel Dennett, who suggest that religion can be explained as adaptations that were selected for in an evolutionary process, and Scott Atran, Justin Barrett and Pascal Boyer, who take religiosity to be a non-adaptive by-product (spandrel) of other adaptive traits. Wilson believes that religion was evolutionarily adaptive by intensifying within-group cooperation and that it evolved via group selection.[23] Dennett's meme theory, too, suggests that religiosity has been promoted through selection, but the selection process is cultural rather than genetic (hence 'meme' rather than 'gene'), and the promotion of religious memes does not necessarily benefit the memes' hosts. Religious memes – ideas, practices, symbols etc. – are adaptive in that they possess features that make these memes likely to spread among the host population. In this sense, rather than to benefit the host, religious traits possess their own fitness qua cultural replicators.[24] The by-product theory as advocated by Atran, Barrett and Boyer regards religious belief as not itself adaptive but as parasitic upon other traits that have been selected by evolution. One idea is that humans are equipped with what has been dubbed a hyperactive agency detection device.[25] This device makes us hypersensitive to agency in that it makes us more likely to mistake an inanimate object for an agent than vice versa. Possessing this trait was adaptive because false negatives are typically more dangerous than false positives. It is better to err on the side of caution mistaking a boulder for a bear than vice versa.[26] And this tendency to 'detect' agents where there are none – to project life onto inanimate objects – provides (at least part of) a wholly naturalistic explanation of people's tendency to believe in supernatural entities. The philosophical implications of the findings from the cognitive science of religion are disputed, and not all advocates of this approach take their findings to have a debunking effect on religious belief. Barrett, for instance, reckons that "theists have nothing to fear from the bio-psychological explanations of religion."[27] Some critics of religion, however, have appealed to such naturalistic explanations of religion in an attempt to undermine religious belief, Daniel Dennett and Richard Dawkins being the most vocal among them.[28]

---

23 D. S. Wilson, 2002.

24 Dennett, 2007. The meme theory is originally due to Dawkins, 1976; see also Dawkins, 2007, pp. 171–207.

25 Barrett, 2000, 2004, see also Atran, 2002; Boyer, 2001.

26 I am borrowing this example from Guthrie, 1993, p. 6.

27 Barrett, 2007, p. 70.

28 Dawkins, 2007; Dennett, 2007.

Debunking arguments have also been applied in metaphysics with the aim of undermining commonsensical views about the nature of ordinary objects. These arguments challenge our folk assumptions about how the world is divided up ontologically. The way we usually conceptually divide up the world – into cats, houses, computers, and so on – reflects our cultural and biological background and is closely tied to our needs as human agents at a particular time and place. For us, such objects as cats, houses and computers have a cultural function qua cats, houses and computers, whereas for instance so called 'incars' – cars that are necessarily in a garage – play no role in our lives. This is why it makes sense for us to carve up the world in such a way that it contains cats, houses, computers but not incars. Debunkers in metaphysics have pointed out that we have no reason to assume that our more or less arbitrary conventions of dividing up the world mirrors how the world is actually ontologically constituted. As Mark Heller observes, "[i]f we accept objects into our ontology because it is convenient, if we conceptually divide up the world into objects one way rather than another because doing so will serve our purposes better, then there is little chance that the resulting ontology will be the true ontology."[29] In light of the arbitrariness of our way of dividing up the world, it would be a great coincidence if it happened to match the actual independent ontological structure of the world.

Finally, debunking arguments have been employed in philosophy of mathematics to cast doubt on mathematical Platonism. Mathematical Platonism is the view that mathematical objects are causally inert abstract entities that existent independently of us and our intellectual activities. If we assume that we can only have knowledge of truths to which we are causally connected, it follows that we have no mathematical knowledge. The initial plausibility of mathematical beliefs is undermined by reflection on what causes these beliefs (or, for that matter, what does *not* cause these beliefs). If mathematical skepticism strikes us implausible, the debunking argument entails a refutation of mathematical Platonism.[30]

In the remainder of this typology, I focus mainly on debunking arguments in moral and political philosophy. But it is worth keeping in mind that there are other arenas in which debunking debates are carried out.[31]

---

29 Heller, 1990, pp. 44; see also for instance Hawthorne, 2006, p. 109; Sider, 2001, pp. 156–157; for a general discussion, refer to Korman, 2014.

30 The problem was originally formulated by Benacceraf (1973) and later refined by Field (1989).

31 For more examples of debunking arguments in other subdisciplines, refer to Korman, 2019.

Scope

Debunking arguments differ in scope. That is, they differ with regard to the size of their target. Some debunking arguments are 'local' in that they target a relatively small subset of a certain type of belief. Greene and Singer's debunking of deontology is an example of such a local debunking argument. It is local in that it targets only deontological beliefs while sparing utilitarian beliefs. Debunking arguments in political theory are usually local in scope, too. Political theorists routinely dismiss rival political theories as 'ideological', while they naturally assume that their own preferred political view is free from ideological prejudice. Thus, debunking arguments in political theory typically target only a specific subset of political beliefs.

Other debunking arguments are more sweeping, or 'global'. Both Street's and Joyce's debunking arguments are particularly far-reaching in that they target *all* moral beliefs, be they deontological, utilitarian, or other.[32] I will argue in this book that Joyce's already far-reaching debunking argument can be extended further to encompass prudential beliefs, too. I will outline a debunking argument that is, if you like, even more 'global' than his.[33]

Ambition

Debunking arguments can be more or less ambitious with respect to their epistemic aim. The ambition of what one might call modest debunkers is merely epistemological. They purport to demonstrate that we are not *justified* to believe the targeted doctrine, or that this doctrine is unlikely to be true. They refrain from making the stronger claim that a debunking argument establishes the falsity of the targeted doctrine. Ambitious debunkers, by contrast, intend their debunking arguments to establish the stronger conclusion that the debunked doctrine has been falsified and refuted.[34]

---

32 There is some ambiguity as to whether Street's argument is intended to target only moral beliefs or evaluative beliefs in general. As I explain later, it is preferable to read her as being primarily concerned with moral beliefs and moral realism.

33 The local/global distinction is due to Kahane, 2011. Local debunking arguments are also referred to as 'selective' debunking arguments (see e.g. Sauer, 2018, who also speaks of the 'scope' of debunking arguments).

34 I have adopted Joyce's way of putting it, who speaks of an "epistemological conclusion" (2013d). The terminology might be slightly misleading, though, as there is of course a sense

Joyce is an example of a modest debunker in the above-defined sense (although the scope of his argument, morality in its entirety, is anything but modest). He has been adamant that his evolutionary debunking of morality falls short of establishing that there are no moral facts. His argument is meant to establish an epistemological conclusion – that we are not justified to believe in moral facts – rather than the error-theoretic conclusion that there definitely are no moral facts. And he emphasizes that his conclusion is only provisional in that it does not rule out that evidence of the existence of moral facts can be produced in the future.[35] Recall the above-cited Waterloo thought experiment: If we were to learn that we have been slipped such a pill, we should give up our belief that Napoleon lost Waterloo. It would, however, be premature to conclude that Napoleon did *not* lose Waterloo (which may or may not be true), and it is conceivable that we come across new evidence that he did actually lose Waterloo.

Michael Ruse, by contrast, whose work on the biology of morality anticipated many of the currently discussed themes, has been credited with holding the more ambitious view.[36] It is possible to interpret him as suggesting that awareness of the evolutionary background of our moral sense establishes that there are no (attitude-independent) moral facts. He asserts that "substantive morality is a kind of illusion" and that a "Darwinian approach to ethics leads one to a kind of moral nonrealism."[37] This contrasts with Joyce's insistence that the kind of skepticism his evolutionary argument is intended to establish is compatible with moral realism in that it does not conclusively rule out the existence of moral facts.

Although ambitious debunking arguments are not entirely unheard-of, most contemporary debunkers are happy to concede that their arguments establish only a modest conclusion. Street, Greene and Singer, too, draw relatively modest conclusions, in that they conclude that it would be *unlikely* that the targeted beliefs are correct. They do not conclude that they are definitively wrong given what we know about the genealogy of these beliefs.[38]

---

in which more ambitious debunking arguments are 'epistemological', too. On this distinction, see also Das, 2016; Lutz, 2018, p. 1106; Wielenberg, 2010.

35 See e.g. Joyce, 2013b, pp. 142–143.

36 Braddock, 2017, p. 2; Joyce, 2013d, p. 356; 2016c, p. 144; Leibowitz and Sinclair, 2017, p. 211.

37 Ruse, 2006, p. 21; see also Ruse, 1986, pp. 252–256.

38 See e.g. Greene, 2008, p. 72; Street, 2006, p. 122.

Level of defeat

The reason why debunking arguments are generally held to entail only such a relatively weak conclusion is that they rely on undercutting defeat. Rather than to give us reason to believe the negation of a proposition, as rebutting defeaters do, they show that the grounds on which a proposition is believed do not in fact support this proposition. The way a debunking argument debunks is by undermining the evidence in support of some proposition rather than by providing evidence against the proposition.[39]

Although all debunking arguments involve undercutting defeaters, different debunking arguments deploy different types of undercutting defeaters. Some debunking arguments involve ordinary undercutting defeaters. Singer and Greene's attack on deontological intuitions is a case in point. It is supposed to show that, contrary to appearance, our deontological intuitions do not support deontology.

Other debunking arguments rely on what has come to be called higher-order defeat. Higher-order evidence is evidence *about* (first-order) evidence. Higher-order defeat involves evidence to the effect that the first-order evidence has not been accurately assessed. Like ordinary undercutting defeat, higher-order defeat "attacks the connection between the evidence and the conclusion, rather than attacking the conclusion itself."[40] Unlike ordinary undercutting defeat, however, higher-order defeat implies that it was never rational to hold the belief in light of the first-order evidence to begin with. Many political debunking arguments are (arguably) based on higher-order evidence.[41] They are supposed to discredit political opponents as being under the sway of some sort of ideological delusion, which has rendered them incapable of correctly assessing the available evidence. Greene and Singer, too, advance a debunking argument that is based on higher-order evidence, alongside their attack on deontological intuitions, which relies on ordinary undercutting defeat.

I will later return to the difference between these two levels of defeat and criticize debunking arguments that rely on higher-order evidence. As we shall

---

39 See e. g. Clarke-Doane, 2016; Clarke-Doane and Baras, 2021; Hofmann, 2018, p. 403; Kahane, 2011, p. 106; Lutz, 2018; Sauer, 2018, p. 29; on defeaters, see Grundmann, 2011; Pollock, 1986, pp. 38 – 39.

40 As Feldman points out (2005, p. 113). The quotation is Pollock's characterization of (regular) undercutting defeat (1986, p. 39). By understanding higher-order defeat as a non-standard type of undercutting defeat, I am following e. g. Christensen, 2010, though this is to some extent a purely terminological issue (Feldman, 2005, p. 113).

41 Whether they are based on higher-order evidence is to some extent a question of interpretation. I return to this issue in Chapter 5.

see, paying attention to this difference will allow us to understand why Searle and many others have been so critical of the genealogical method.[42]

Reason for defeat

The general idea behind debunking arguments is that the genealogical story that features in a debunking argument reveals that the targeted beliefs have not originated from a truth-tracking process. It would therefore be a massive coincidence if these beliefs turned out true. Evidence of this constitutes an undercutting defeater, undermining the justification of these beliefs. While this much is common ground among debunkers, they can say, and have said, different things about how exactly the debunking conclusion follows from the genealogical premise, that is, about why the genealogical story provides an undercutting defeater.

Some debunkers seem to hold that a debunking explanation provides an undercutting defeater by revealing the targeted beliefs to be insensitive to the truth. Someone's belief that p is insensitive if she would still believe that p even if p were actually false. At least at one point, for instance, Joyce, writes:

> Suppose that the actual world contains real categorical requirements – the kind that would be necessary to render moral discourse true. In such a world humans will be disposed to make moral judgments [...], for natural selection will make it so. Now imagine instead that the actual world contains no such requirements at all – nothing to make moral discourse true. In such a world humans will *still* be disposed to make these judgments [...], just as they did in the first world, for natural selection will make it so. What this shows is that the process that generates moral judgments exhibits an independence relation between judgment and truth, and these judgments are thus unjustified.[43]

Similarly, Ruse observes that "[y]ou would believe what you do about right and wrong, irrespective of whether or not a 'true' right and wrong existed!"[44] While sensitivity is usually discussed as a condition for knowledge, the idea here is that information that a belief lacks a condition for knowledge (sensitivity) provides

---

42 Defeaters play a role not only in internalist but also in externalist epistemology. Most externalists adopt a no-defeater condition, according to which the subject must not have any evidence that defeats the belief (e.g. Goldman, 1986, pp. 62–63; Nozick, 1981, p. 196; Plantinga, 1993, pp. 40–42; see also Grundmann, 2009).

43 2001, p. 163; though see 2016e, p. 132.

44 Ruse, 1986, p. 254. Kahane, too, characterizes debunking arguments as being about lack of sensitivity (2011, p. 106; see Bogardus, 2016, p. 639).

an undercutting defeater of justification.[45] There are several problems with this line of thinking. One is that the sensitivity condition has implausibly skeptical implications when applied in other domains. For example, the belief that we are not brains in a vat fails to be sensitive, as we would still have this belief if we were brains in a vat. Another is that the sensitivity condition has problems handling beliefs about metaphysically necessary truths. This is particularly problematic for debunking arguments in moral philosophy, as moral truths are typically thought to be metaphysically necessary truths. It means that our true moral beliefs would trivially meet the sensitivity condition because there is no world in which the counterfactual's antecedent ("if p were actually false") is true.[46]

An alternative and more promising modal interpretation of the logic of debunking arguments is that they show that the targeted beliefs fail to be safe, rather than that they fail to be sensitive. Here, in order for our beliefs to be safe, it must be the case that we could not easily have had false beliefs. According to this approach, what debunking explanations do is to provide evidence that we could easily have had false beliefs. Again, the assumption is that information about the lack of safety, which is a condition for knowledge, constitutes an undercutting defeater. Moral truths being metaphysically necessary truths, the idea must be that moral debunking arguments show that we could easily have had different (and thus false) moral beliefs from the ones we actually have, rather than that the moral facts could easily have been different.[47] These beliefs would then fail to meet the safety condition. It has variously been suggested that this is exactly what evolutionary genealogies of moral beliefs achieve. Evolution could easily have followed a different trajectory, in which case we would have winded up with different (false) moral beliefs than the ones we actually hold: "[T]here are nearby worlds where our evolutionary history took slightly different turns and we arrived at radically different moral views using the same cognitive faculties that we used in the actual world, and these views are, of course,

---

45 The sensitivity condition on knowledge is due to Nozick (1981).

46 These and further objections have been suggested by Bogardus, 2016; Braddock, 2017; Clarke-Doane, 2016; 2020, pp. 104–108; Cowie, 2020; Leibowitz and Sinclair, 2017; Srinivasan, 2015; White, 2010. Note that Braddock has defended an improved debunking argument from insensitivity (2017).

47 See Clarke-Doane, 2016, p. 28. This is why Srinivasan offers the following formulation of the safety condition: "S's belief in the necessary proposition p is safe$_n$ iff S could not have easily believed not-p using a sufficiently similar method she uses to believe p." (2015, p. 339) It thus differs from Sosa's formulation of the safety condition on knowledge (Sosa, 1999). On the two different ways in which a belief can be unsafe, see also Clarke-Doane, 2020, p. 108; Clarke-Doane and Baras, 2021.

false".[48] Critics have disputed this claim, insisting that there is no nearby world in which evolution would not have inclined us to hold the moral beliefs we actually hold, such as, say, that we ought to care for our children.[49]

Another way of fleshing out the epistemic principle informing debunking arguments is to interpret such arguments as showing that there is no plausible explanation of the reliability of the process that generates the targeted beliefs. Street can be read as advancing a debunking argument along these lines. In light of the evolutionary origins of our moral beliefs, there is no plausible explanation of how our moral faculty could possibly be reliable. Its reliability would be a huge coincidence, a mere fluke, at least if we assume a realist meta-ethical framework.[50] In response to this challenge, realists have provided so-called third-factor accounts, which are supposed to explain the reliability of our moral faculty. Third-factor accounts posit a factor that explains the correlation between our moral beliefs and the direction in which evolutionary forces have pushed us. The preferred strategy is to argue that it was adaptive to have correct moral beliefs because of what the moral truth *actually is*. David Enoch, for instance, suggests: "Selective forces have shaped our normative judgments and beliefs, with the 'aim' of survival or reproductive success in mind (so to speak). But given that these are by-and-large good aims — aims that normative truths recommend — our normative beliefs have developed to be at least somewhat in line with the normative truths."[51] According to third-factor accounts like Enoch's, our moral faculty did not evolve *in order to* track the moral truth, but it evolved in such a way that it ended up tracking it nonetheless. Third-factor accounts are controversial, as they tend to presuppose the truth of some moral judgements, a move that has struck many as question-begging.[52]

Yet another idea is that a debunking explanation provides an undercutting defeater by showing that it would be ontologically profligate to posit the existence of the facts that the targeted beliefs are about. This seems to be Joyce's preferred rationale for dismissing people's belief in moral facts in light of the evolu-

---

48 Barkhausen, 2016, p. 681. See also Joyce, 2016e; Ruse and Wilson, 1985; Srinivasan, 2015.
49 Clarke-Doane, 2016; 2020, pp. 109–110; Cowie, 2020. For criticism of the safety approach, see also Bogardus, 2016; Leibowitz and Sinclair, 2017.
50 Street, 2006.
51 Enoch, 2010, p. 430. Other champions of third-factor accounts include Behrends, 2013; Brosnan, 2011; Copp, 2008; Schafer, 2010; Skarsaune, 2011; Wielenberg, 2010. For discussions of third-factor accounts, see Berker, 2014; Klenk, 2020; Morton, 2018b.
52 Dyke, 2020; Joyce, 2014, 2016c; Street, 2008b, 2016. For discussions of this problem, see Copp, 2019; Morton, 2018b. See Behrends, 2013 for a third-factor account that does not invoke substantive moral truths.

tionary background of this belief. The evolutionary story of how we have come to believe in the existence of moral facts does not make any reference to such facts, at least if we assume that moral facts are not reducible to the natural facts featuring in this story. Moral facts ought therefore to be removed from our ontology on grounds of ontological parsimony. They are explanatorily superfluous and can be excised using Ockham's Razor.[53] By the same token, one might argue that if we have a compelling naturalistic explanation of religious belief, it would be ontologically profligate to posit the existence of a god. One question mark hovers over the ambition of this debunking approach. Joyce professes to be a modest debunker, seeking only to undermine the justification of our moral beliefs. But talk of ontological parsimony and Ockham's Razor may seem more compatible with an ambitious, metaphysical reading, according to which the argument shows that the relevant (e.g. moral) properties do not exist, rather than just that our belief in them is unjustified.[54] Also, this way of understanding the epistemic principle behind debunking arguments may again have implausibly skeptical implications. It is at least questionable whether, say, mathematical, logical or, indeed, philosophical properties feature in the best explanations of our mathematical, logical and philosophical beliefs, given that necessary truths are arguably causally inert.[55]

How, or perhaps if, debunking explanations, evolutionary or other, succeed at undermining the justification of the targeted beliefs is still a matter of some controversy. But it is fair to say that the epistemic intuition that is driving debunking arguments is extremely compelling, and epistemological theorizing about debunking arguments should at least to some extent attempt to accommodate this intuition. If our best account of undercutting defeat fails to account for this intuition, this might just point to a flaw in our account of undercutting defeat.

One promising attempt to make sense of how evolutionary debunking arguments succeed at doing their undermining work has recently been outlined by Michael Klenk in response to a skeptical perspective on genealogical debunking offered by Dan Baras and Justin Clarke-Doane. The latter have suggested that 1) evolutionary and other classical debunking arguments fail to show that the targeted beliefs are insensitive or unsafe (for reasons mentioned above), and 2) that modal insecurity, that is, lack of sensitivity or safety, is a necessary condition on undercutting defeat. Debunking a belief by means of undercutting de-

---

53 Joyce, 2006, ch. 6; see also Street, 2006, p. 129. Joyce's reasoning is inspired by Harman, 1977.
54 See Lutz, 2018, p. 1106 n2.
55 Srinivasan, 2015, p. 332. For other problems see e.g. FitzPatrick, 2015; White, 2010, pp. 582–585; Wielenberg, 2010, pp. 461–463.

feat requires showing that it lacks either sensitivity or safety. This would entail that evolutionary and other classic debunking arguments fail. Again, sensitivity and safety being conditions for knowledge rather than justification, the additional assumption here is that if a piece of information, for example about the genealogy of a belief, does not give you reason to doubt that this belief satisfies the conditions for knowledge, it does not defeat its justification.[56]

As Klenk observes, however, virtue epistemologists have plausibly suggested that for a true belief to qualify as knowledge, its being true must be creditable to the cognitive abilities of the epistemic agent. Knowledge, on this view, is a kind of epistemic achievement. There are true beliefs that are safe or both safe and sensitive that intuitively strike out as falling short of knowledge precisely because their being true is not attributable to the epistemic agent's cognitive abilities. This implies that modal insecurity (lack of sensitivity or safety) is not a necessary condition on undercutting defeat. One can instead undermine a belief by showing that its being true would not be due to any cognitive abilities on the part of the epistemic agent, as this is a condition on knowledge. Debunkers can exploit this finding and argue that genealogies can defeat the justification of a belief by showing that, if the belief were true, its being true could not be credited to the epistemic agent (rather than by showing it to be either unsafe or insensitive).[57]

Dialectical function

Genealogical debunking explanations can have different dialectical functions. By this I mean that they differ with regard to what their authors aim to achieve by providing them. I suggest that we distinguish between debunking arguments proper, supporting debunking arguments, and mere genealogical diagnoses.

Let us first consider the default case, debunking arguments proper. A debunking argument proper is an independent challenge to the justification of a belief or doctrine. Greene and Singer's debunking of deontology may serve as an example of this type of debunking challenge. It is independent in that it is not intended as a mere appendix to a 'regular' (non-debunking) argument against deontology or for utilitarianism, although it may of course accompany such regular arguments.

---

56 Clarke-Doane and Baras, 2021; see also Clarke-Doane, 2015, 2020.
57 Klenk, forthcoming.

Contrast this with how supporting debunking arguments work. A supporting debunking argument is intended by its author to deal with the fact that people disagree with the conclusion of a regular argument advanced by the same author. Huemer's debunking explanation of popular belief in the rightfulness of state power is an example of such a supporting debunking argument. He takes popular opinion, which is overwhelmingly anti-anarcho-capitalist, to speak against the correctness of his argument for anarcho-capitalism. As he observes, "[a]nyone who holds an unpopular view can be challenged to answer, 'How have so many others gone wrong, while you have avoided their error?' This question should be taken seriously."[58] Huemer's response is that there exist a range of psychological biases that cloud people's judgment on these issues, and this defuses the problem that popular opinion is not on his side. This debunking argument is thus put forth as a necessary supplement to a regular argument, rather than as a free-standing debunking argument in its own right.[59]

Finally, there are what I have called genealogical diagnoses. A genealogical diagnosis resembles a debunking explanation in that it involves a critical genealogical account of how a mistaken doctrine has come to be accepted.[60] However, genealogical diagnoses are offered only after the falsity of the relevant doctrine has already been conclusively established. They provide an account of the psychological biases or prejudices that explain the endorsement of this doctrine, but they are not themselves meant to cast doubt on this doctrine. Indeed, genealogical diagnoses are not supposed to do any argumentative work at all. They are dispensable to the argument itself and only of psychological or historical interest. One example of such a genealogical diagnosis is Jason Brennan and Peter Jaworski's explanation of why people oppose the commodification of certain goods, such as organs, surrogacy and sex.[61] First, they argue that goods like these should be allowed to be commercially traded. Then, in a second step, they speculate that people oppose markets in such goods because they are overcome by a feeling of disgust when they think about it. This second step serves as a purely descriptive analysis of why people are mistaken about the permissibility of commercializing certain goods. Its omission would not weaken their argument.

---

58 Huemer, 2013, p. 134.
59 Debunking arguments of this sort are discussed in Ballantyne, 2015.
60 Similarly, Mason distinguishes diagnostic arguments and debunking arguments (2011, p. 771). If prefer the term 'genealogical diagnoses' over 'diagnostic arguments', as genealogical diagnoses do not function as arguments at all.
61 Brennan and Jaworski, 2015, 2016.

In many other cases, the precise function of a debunking explanation remains elusive. Often, when a genealogical account of how a certain mistaken doctrine has come to be believed is offered, it remains unclear whether this genealogy is supposed to work as a debunking argument or to be only of psychological or historical interest. Nozick's above mentioned debunking explanation of why intellectuals tend to despise capitalism is a case in point. While it is tempting to read it as a debunking argument proper, designed to undermine opposition to libertarianism, its dialectical purpose is left unspecified by Nozick. It might as well be intended as a supporting debunking argument or, indeed, as piece of purely descriptive psychological analysis that does not purport to exert any argumentative pressure.

Direction

Finally, the direction of debunking arguments may differ. The default case is that a debunking argument is put forth in an attempt to challenge the view of a philosophical opponent. The argument is in this case directed against other people's convictions rather than one's own. Utilitarians try to debunk deontology, error theorists try to debunk belief in moral facts, libertarians try to debunk the anti-capitalist mentality, communists try to debunk the free-market 'ideology', and so forth. It is worth pointing out, though, that one may also engage in genealogical self-criticism. Rather than to debunk one's opponent's convictions, genealogical inquiry may lead one to conclude that one's own views rest on shaky foundations. One notable, and perhaps laudable, example of such a self-directed debunking argument has been provided by the late G.A. Cohen. Cohen, one of the leading figures of contemporary analytical Marxism, suspects that his communist inclinations can be explained away as the outcome of his upbringing in a Jewish working-class neighborhood of Montreal.[62] Although Cohen admits to being unsure whether this debunking explanation is sound or not, his argument may serve as an illustration of how the genealogical method can be used in a self-directed and self-critical fashion.

---

62 Cohen, 2000, ch. 1; for discussions, see Vavova, 2018; White, 2010.

1.3 Aims and structure of this book

This book explores the nature, significance and limitations of moral debunking arguments. Each chapter is devoted to one moral debunking argument, or one aspect of a moral debunking argument. Chapters 2 to 5 discuss aspects of the attempted debunking of deontology. Chapter 6 explores the idea that evolutionary considerations vindicate moral constructivism. And Chapter 7 revolves around evolutionary debunking arguments that focus on normative concepts, moral and prudential, rather than the contents of our normative judgments.

The chapters of this book are to some extent autonomous, each exploring one debunking project. At the same time, the chapters of this book are united by common themes. The most important theme, which runs through the entire book, is what I call the backfiring problem.[63] I will argue that each of the moral debunking arguments under consideration backfires in the sense that it challenges, in one way or other, the debunker's own preferred moral or metaethical position. The methods used to debunk deontology threaten to undermine utilitarianism. (Chapters 2 and 3). The attempted Darwinian vindication of constructivism backfires in that the Darwinian argument really suggests that we should become skeptics about morality rather than (Humean) constructivists (Chapter 6). And the evolutionary debunking argument of morality collapses into skepticism about both morality and prudential normativity, destroying the prospect of defending morality as a useful fiction on prudential grounds (Chapter 7).

This theme can thus be summarized in three principal claims.

1) Once we assume that *some* moral convictions have an evolutionary background, it is likely that these include not only deontological ones but also some that are central to utilitarianism. Similarly, once we embark on exploring which factors our moral intuitions are sensitive to, we will likely find that both deontological and utilitarian intuitions are sensitive to morally irrelevant factors. Thus, neither approach will vindicate utilitarianism.

2) Once we assume that evolutionary forces have messed with virtually *all* of our moral commitments, we should become skeptics about morality rather than (Humean) constructivists.

3) Once we assume that evolution has generated our normative *concepts*, it is natural to assume that this applies not only to our moral but also our pru-

---

63 Certain manifestations of this problem have been referred to as the 'tu quoque problem' (Shafer-Landau, 2012, p. 13; I have myself used this term in print) and 'the generalization problem' (Rini, 2016).

dential concepts, which means that we should become skeptics not only about morality but also about wellbeing.

In a way, each step supersedes the previous one(s). If we assume that evolution has messed with virtually all our moral commitments, the utilitarian debunking project is obviously a non-starter. Likewise, if we are not justified to believe in any moral facts to begin with, attempts to establish moral constructivism or utilitarianism are futile. But I take it that each of the three principal claims are interesting in their own right, especially as there is no consensus about the precise impact of evolution on our moral cognition. There is disagreement about whether evolution has shaped some moral convictions or the bulk of them, or, indeed, whether evolution might account for our very thinking in moral concepts. Each part of the three-part narrative accepts different starting points, so to speak, and explores their implications.

A minor common theme, which connects three of the chapters on the debunking of deontology, is the scope problem. It refers to the problem that the anti-deontological debunking effort fails to pose a threat to more than just a small selection of deontological judgments.

While much of the debate surrounding debunking arguments has focused on the epistemological intricacies of these arguments, the narrative arch of this book revolves around the dialectical implications of debunking arguments in ethics. One principal takeaway of my investigation will be that moral debunking arguments tend to be both too destructive and too weak at the same time. They are too destructive in that they undermine the debunker's own moral or metaethical views. And at least the anti-deontological debunking program is also too weak in that it fails to pose a serious threat to more than just a relatively minor proportion of deontological judgments.

2 Deontology, Utilitarianism, and Evolution

2.1 Introduction

This book explores three different debunking projects in ethics: One that targets deontological judgments, one that seeks to undermine moral realism, and one that targets belief in moral facts in general. Of these three debunking attempts, the debunking argument against deontology, developed by Greene and Singer, is the most circumscribed one in that it targets only a subset of people's moral beliefs (deontological ones) while sparing others (utilitarian ones). But it is arguably the most complex, and at times confusing, of the existing debunking projects in ethics. The complexity is due both to the two-layered structure of the argument and to the fact that there is more than one version of this argument.

The argument has a two-layered structure in that it consists of two debunking arguments that complement each other. I will refer to them as the primary and secondary argument. The primary argument targets our deontological intuitions. Its purpose is to cast doubt on our knee-jerk deontological gut reactions. The secondary argument targets more sophisticated deontological theories, which are not justified by appeal to the intuitions that are targeted by the primary argument. These more sophisticated deontological theories are dismissed as products of confabulatory post hoc rationalization. Both the primary and the secondary argument are debunking arguments. Together they form a larger, composite debunking argument.

There is more than just one version of this debunking argument, because the primary argument is open to at least three different interpretations. According to one interpretation, our deontological intuitions must be distrusted because they are products of natural selection. This argument is similar to Street's, except that it focuses specifically on deontological intuitions. I will refer to this interpretation as the argument from evolutionary history. According to a second interpretation, we must distrust our deontological intuitions because they are responsive to factors that lack moral significance. This is the argument from moral irrelevance. Finally, according to a third interpretation, deontological intuitions should be dismissed as dysfunctional on the grounds of their genealogy. The suggested genealogy has both evolutionary and non-evolutionary components. On this interpretation, the primary argument asserts that we will fail to overcome our moral problems as long as we rely blindly on our deontological gut reactions. I will call this version the functionalist argument.

The complete debunking argument must be interpreted as a combination of at least one version of the primary argument plus the argument from confabula-

https://doi.org/10.1515/9783110750195-003

The primary argument (targets deontological intuitions)	1. The argument from evolutionary history (especially de Lazari-Radek and Singer, 2012; Greene, 2008; Singer, 2005)	2. The argument from moral irrelevance (especially Greene, 2010, 2013, 2014, 2016)	3. The functionalist argument (especially Greene, 2010, 2013, 2014, 2017)
The secondary argument (targets elaborate deontological theories)		The argument from confabulation (especially Greene, 2008, 2013, 2014; Singer, 2005)	

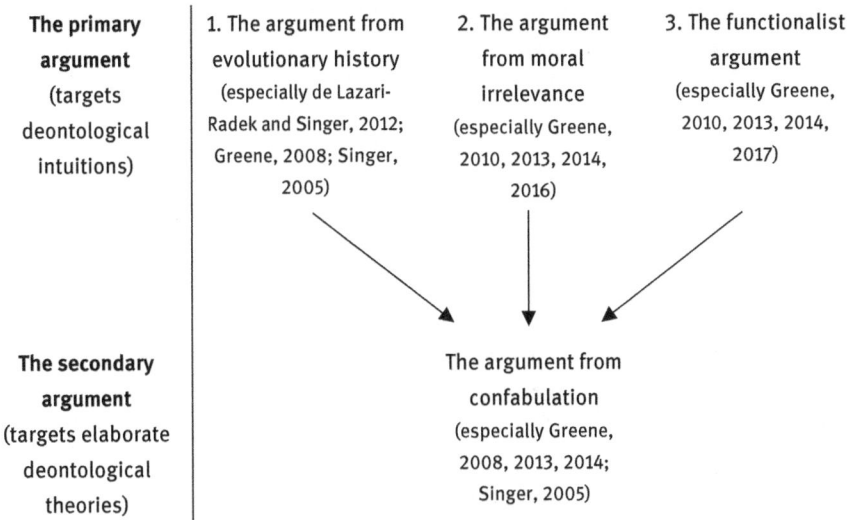

Fig. 1: The structure of the anti-deontological debunking project

tion. In this and the following chapters, I will engage with each of these four sub-arguments in turn, examine their merits, and explore what these debunking attempts can teach us about the prospects of the anti-deontological debunking project, the significance of experimental ethics, and the argumentation-theoretical status of debunking arguments.[64]

Although combining into one composite debunking argument, each of these sub-arguments constitutes an interesting debunking project in its own right, which is worth assessing on its own terms and the assessment of which will yield insights of more general relevance. The purpose of these chapters is thus not just to examine the soundness of the anti-deontological debunking project, but to contribute to a better general understanding of the nature and value of debunking arguments and empirically informed ethics. In the present chapter, I introduce the backfiring problem, which will be taken up in later chapters of this book and which constitutes the most formidable problem for would-be de-

---

64 Helpful for understanding the structure of the anti-deontological debunking project are Berker, 2009 and Paulo, 2019. Greene and Singer's own writings are to some extent indeterminate with respect to the precise architecture of the overall argument. Singer appears to favor the argument from evolutionary history over the two alternatives. Greene used to favor the argument from evolutionary history, but he now seems to endorse the argument from moral irrelevance alongside the functionalist argument (which he does not always distinguish). Both have endorsed the argument from confabulation.

bunkers. Chapter 3 provides lessons about the philosophical value of findings from experimental ethics. Chapter 4 reveals the pitfalls of construing morality as a means to an end. And in Chapter 5, I use the argument from confabulation as a point of departure to distinguish two kinds of debunking arguments and to reflect on their respective admissibility within and outside academic ethical inquiry.

2.2 The dual-process account of moral judgment

Central to the anti-deontological debunking project is Greene's dual-process account of moral judgment, according to which our moral cognition operates in two different modes. There is a fast, automatic, emotion-driven mode of forming moral judgments, which is evolutionarily old, and a slower, more 'cognitive' one, which is evolutionarily recent. The dual-process account builds upon the social-intuitionist model developed by Jonathan Haidt. The central claim of Haidt's model is that, typically, "moral judgement is caused by quick moral intuitions and is followed (when needed) by slow, ex post facto moral reasoning."[65] Moral reasoning usually takes place only after the moral judgment has been made and tends to be confabulatory. People are often unable to name the reasons that their moral judgment is actually based upon and provide instead an entirely fabricated story of how they have formed the moral judgment.

In the now famous 'dumbfounding' experiment, participants were asked to judge whether it was morally OK for two siblings, Julie and Mark, to have protected, consensual sex. It was stipulated that they enjoyed making love and that they decided not to do it again and not to tell anyone about it. In short, it was stipulated that nobody was or will be harmed. Participants would immediately reply that their behavior was not morally OK, but they struggled to explain why. They would offer justifications that were directly contradicted by the description of the scenario, mentioning e. g. the risks associated with inbreeding or the possibility of emotional distress.[66] Interestingly, while Haidt believes that ordinary people rarely 'reason' their way to moral convictions, he takes professional moral philosophers to be more likely to resist the temptation to engage in post hoc rationalization.[67]

---

65 Haidt, 2001, p. 817. I am here mentioning only two of the six components of Haidt's model.
66 Haidt, 2001; Haidt et al., 2000.
67 Haidt, 2001, p. 819.

Haidt's model is, by and large, accepted by Greene and Singer as an accurate account of how deontological judgments are formed but rejected as an account of consequentialist judgment. While deontologists are portrayed as post hoc rationalizers of deontological gut reactions, utilitarians are credited with reaching their utilitarian judgments through relatively slow and thoughtful reasoning. The dual-process account is thus 'dual' in that is posits two different mechanisms responsible for moral judgment, one for deontological judgments and one for utilitarian ones. It holds that "[c]haracteristically deontological judgments are preferentially supported by automatic emotional responses, while characteristically consequentialist judgments are preferentially supported by conscious reasoning and allied processes of cognitive control."[68] Consequentialist judgments are defined as those that are most naturally justified by appeal to the utilitarian principle of impartially maximizing good consequences, deontological ones as those that are hard to justify in consequentialist terms and more easily justifiable by appeal to such deontological concepts as 'rights', 'duties', etc.[69, 70]

The notion that our cognition operates in two different modes is anything but new. The dual-process approach to human cognition is among the most influential and comprehensive research programs in recent psychological research. Dual-process theories have been proposed in a wide array of fields, including learning, reasoning, social cognition and decision-making.[71] Greene's dual-process theory is an application of this widely accepted paradigm to the domain of moral judgment. Given the currency of dual-process theories, the idea that moral judgment operates in two different modes is, as Greene acknowledges, not particularly innovative. The innovative bit is the suggestion that these two modes correspond to different types of moral judgments, namely deontological and consequentialist ones.[72] Greene's model, just like Haidt's, also forms part of the larger research program that stresses the intuitive and emotional dimension of moral cognition, parting ways with the long-dominant rationalist paradigm associated with Jean Piaget and Lawrence Kohlberg.[73]

---

68 Greene, 2014, p. 699.
69 Greene, 2008, pp. 38–39; 2014, p. 699. Whether consequentialist/utilitarian responses to sacrificial dilemmas indicate a commitment to the utilitarian ideal of impartial concern for the greater good has been disputed (Kahane, 2012, 2014b, 2015; Kahane et al., 2015, 2018; Kahane and Shackel, 2010; Wiech et al., 2013; though see Conway et al., 2018).
70 While there are consequentialist theories other than utilitarianism, consequentialism and utilitarianism will be used synonymously.
71 Evans, 2008, 2011.
72 Greene, 2014, pp. 698–699.
73 Kohlberg, 1969; Piaget, 1997, p. 13. For a review of recent developments, see Cushman et al., 2010, pp. 47–48.

The most important evidence for the dual-process account of moral judgment comes from Greene and colleagues' studies on differences between deontological and consequentialist responses to different sacrificial dilemmas, such as different variations of the notorious trolley dilemma. The trolley dilemma is a thought experiment designed to test our intuitions about the moral permissibility of causing the death of one person in order to save several others. It features a runaway trolley that is headed for five workers on the tracks, who will be killed unless the trolley is stopped or redirected, but stopping or redirecting the trolley costs the life of an innocent bystander. In the *Switch* version one can hit a switch to redirect the trolley onto a second track, where it will run over one person rather than five. In *Loop*, the side track with only one worker on it loops back onto the main track towards the five people further down the track.[74] If the trolley is diverted onto the side track, the person on the side track stops the trolley, preventing it from running over the five persons further along on the main track. In the *Footbridge* version, one has the option of shoving a heavy person off a footbridge onto the trolley tracks below, which will kill the heavy person but also stop the trolley from running over the five workers further down the tracks.

The trolley dilemma was originally devised by Philippa Foot, adapted and popularized by Judith Jarvis Thomson, and has eventually spawned a large body of 'trolleyological' research devoted to exploring and making sense of our responses to different versions of the dilemma.[75] In particular, trolleyologists have struggled to understand why some ways of sacrificing one person for five others (e. g. in *Switch*) strike us as permissible and others (e. g. in *Footbridge*) do not.

Greene and colleagues have approached this question empirically. Instead of contenting themselves with testing normative intuitions introspectively from the philosopher's armchair, he and his colleagues tested people's responses to trolley dilemmas and other sacrificial dilemmas experimentally, collecting fMRI and reaction time data.

In one study, they hypothesized that the reason why similar sacrificial dilemmas elicit different moral intuitions is that they cause different degrees of emotional engagement in the respondent. When a dilemma engages us emotionally, it elicits a deontological intuition; when it does not, it tends to elicit utilitarian responses. They further hypothesized that whether or not a dilemma engages us emotionally depends on whether it involves 'up close and personal' violations.

---

74 To be precise, according to Thomson's description of *Loop*, there is literally a loop rather than a sidetrack that connects back to the main track. But these two versions of *Loop* are typically regarded as morally equivalent in the literature.

75 Foot, 1967; Thomson, 1976. For one helpful overview, see Bruers and Braeckman, 2014. For a critique of the trolleyological research program, refer to Sauer, 2018, ch. 6.

The *Footbridge* version, for instance, involves 'up close and personal' violations, whereas *Switch* is an impersonal version of the dilemma. Greene and colleagues had their participants respond to dilemmas that were classified as either 'up close and personal' (*Footbridge*-like) or 'impersonal' (*Switch*-like), and they found that brain areas associated with emotional activity were more active when participants contemplated the former, and brain areas associated with abstract reasoning and problem-solving showed increased activity when participants contemplated the latter.[76]

This evidence for dual-process theory was expanded by a follow-up study, in which Greene and colleagues tested two hypotheses derived from the above study. First, they tested the conjecture that longer reaction times to personal dilemmas are really due to a conflict between a prepotent emotional response and more 'cognitive' processing mechanisms. To test this, they subdivided the set of personal dilemmas into two subclasses: high-reaction-time personal dilemmas and low-reaction-time personal dilemmas. An example of the former is *Crying Baby:* In a war, you and a couple of fellow villagers are hiding from enemy troops that are raiding the village. Your baby starts to cry, and you cover its mouth to prevent it from giving away your position. If you remove your hand, the enemy soldiers will find you and kill everyone (including the baby). If you do not remove your hand, your baby will suffocate, but everyone else survives. This dilemma causes long reaction times because there are good reasons to overrule the initial emotional impulse to avoid killing a baby. An example of the latter is *Infanticide*, which involves a teenage mother who considers killing her unwanted newborn child. This is a low-reaction-time dilemma as there is little to be said in favor of killing an infant just because it is unwanted, and there is therefore no conflict between the intuitive emotional response and possible countervailing considerations. Greene and colleagues hypothesized that high-reaction-time personal dilemmas (like *Crying Baby*) lead to increased activity of brain regions associated with cognitive conflicts and with cognitive control and abstract reasoning processes, as compared to low-reaction-time personal dilemmas (like *Infanticide*). Second, they tested whether a brain area that is associated with more controlled reasoning processes is responsible for consequentialist responses to high-reaction-time personal dilemmas. Their prediction was that increased activity in this brain area increases the likelihood of consequentialist responses to these dilemmas.

---

76 Greene et al., 2001. They also collected reaction-time data in this study, which were, however, incorrectly interpreted (Greene, 2009; McGuire et al., 2009).

In their previous study, it had only been shown that different types of dilemmas (personal vs. impersonal dilemmas) engage different brain areas, but it had not been shown that different patterns of neural activity in response to the same class of dilemmas (high-reaction-time personal dilemmas) are correlated with different responses. Both hypotheses were found to be supported. According to Greene and colleagues, these findings indicate that people who take longer when giving a positive answer to high-reaction-time moral dilemmas take longer because they engage in cognitive deliberation overruling the initial emotional deontological response in favor of a consequentialist judgment.

These two studies are the founding studies of dual-process theory, providing some of the most important and spectacular evidence for this theory. But there is a plethora of other findings pointing in a similar direction.[77] Both the argument from evolutionary history and the functionalist argument appeal to the dual-process theory, whereas the dependence of the argument from moral irrelevance on dual-process theory is, as we shall see, doubtful.

2.3 The argument from evolutionary history

According to the argument from evolutionary history, deontological responses are to be distrusted because of their evolutionary origin:

The Argument from Evolutionary History

P1) Our deontological intuitions are products of evolution.

P2) The forces of evolution do not track the attitude-independent moral truth.

P3) If our deontological intuitions are products of forces that do not track the attitude-independent moral truth, they do not have any genuine normative force.

C) Deontological intuitions do not have any genuine normative force.[78]

---

77 Including Greene et al. 2008; Shenhav and Greene, 2014. For a more complete overview of the evidence for dual-process theory, see Greene, 2014, pp. 701–706; Greene and Young, 2020. While the existence of such additional evidence reduces the relevance of criticism specifically of Greene and colleagues' fMRI studies (e.g. Klein, 2011), the general attempt to map the deontology/consequentialism distinction on the emotional(automatic)/cognitive(controlled) distinction has met with skepticism (e.g. Heinzelmann, 2018; Kahane, 2012, 2014b, 2015; Kahane et al., 2012; though see Paxton et al., 2014). More recently, Greene has suggested that the dual-process model of morality can be made sense of in terms of the model-based/model-free distinction (Greene, 2017; see Crockett, 2013; Cushman, 2013).

78 I have modified Berker's account of the argument (2009, p. 319) in order to distinguish it more clearly from the functionalist argument.

The argument targets in particular such deontological intuitions as that there is something objectionable about personal as opposed to impersonal ways of inflicting harm, that we have less of an obligation to faraway people in need than to people in our vicinity, that culpable wrongdoers deserve retributive punishment, and that incest is morally wrong.[79]

Like other evolutionary debunking arguments, this evolutionary debunking of deontological intuitions is premised on the assumption that evolution is not a truth-tracking process. Greene observes that "it is unlikely that inclinations that evolved as evolutionary by-products correspond to some independent, rationally discoverable moral truth."[80] This interpretation of the primary argument is a classic evolutionary debunking argument, which challenges our deontological intuitions on the grounds of their evolutionary genealogy.

Greene and Singer present the dual-process account of moral judgment as being at the heart of the empirically informed attack on deontology. But as formulated above, the argument from evolutionary history does not explicitly mention the dual-process account. If we look closely, however, the dual-process account can be seen to be relevant to the argument from evolutionary history by constituting one of two lines of evidence for the claim that deontological intuitions are products of evolution. P1 is, at least in part, supported by the dual-process account of moral judgment.

But I will begin by explaining the other line evidence. The evolutionary hypothesis is supported directly by considerations concerning whether the targeted deontological disposition may plausibly have been selected by evolution. This includes ad hoc considerations of plausibility. For example, it is plausible that there is an evolutionary explanation of why we have a moral aversion to inflicting harm in an 'up close and personal' fashion but no parallel aversion to inflicting harm in impersonal ways. Personal dilemmas involve the sort of violations that were familiar to our evolutionary ancestors. They involve "those harms that a chimp can understand".[81] Impersonal dilemmas, by contrast, involve violations that were made possible by relatively recent technology and that our ancestors would not have come across. Greene explains:

> It is very likely that we humans have inherited many of our social instincts from our primate ancestors, among them instincts that rein in the tendencies of individuals to harm one another. These instincts are emotional, triggered by behaviors and other elicitors that were present in our ancestral environment. This environment did not include opportunities to

---

79 Greene, 2008; Singer, 2005.
80 Greene, 2008, p. 72.
81 Greene, 2005a, p. 345.

harm other individuals using complicated, remote-acting machinery, but it did include op-
portunities to harm other individuals by pushing them into harms way (e. g. off a cliff or
into a river). Thus, one might suppose that the sorts of basic, interpersonal violence that
threatened our ancestors back then will 'push our buttons' today in a way that peculiarly
modern harms do not.[82]

It was this evolutionary conjecture that motivated the distinction between 'personal' and 'impersonal' dilemmas in the first place.[83] Likewise, Greene and Singer find it plausible that we have evolved to care more about nearby people than
faraway people. It just seems reasonable to assume that these moral dispositions
provided an evolutionary advantage to our ancestors. The considerations that
directly support the evolutionary hypothesis also include more sophisticated evidence, such as mathematical models that demonstrate how altruistic punishment may have been adaptive, explaining our retributive deontological intuitions, or empirical evidence that incest aversion may have naturally evolved.[84]
This first source of evidence for the evolutionary hypothesis does not rely on
dual-process theory. The above explanations do not and need not mention the
finding that deontological responses, unlike consequentialist ones, are emotion-driven.

But dual-process theory provides *additional* evidence for at least some of the
evolutionary claims, constituting the second source of evidence. Emotion-driven
moral responses are assumed to be evolution's preferred method of bringing
about the desired behavioral effect:

> Why should our adaptive moral behavior be driven by moral emotions as opposed to some-
> thing else, such as moral reasoning? The answer, I believe, is that emotions are very reli-
> able, quick, and efficient responses to recurring situations, whereas reasoning is unreliable,
> slow, and inefficient in such contexts. [...] Nature doesn't leave it to us to figure out that
> saving a drowning child is a good thing to do. Instead, it endows us with a powerful
> 'moral sense' that compels us to engage in this sort of behavior (under the right circumstan-
> ces). In short, when Nature needs to get a behavioral job done, it does it with intuition and
> emotion wherever it can. Thus, from an evolutionary point of view, it is no surprise that

---

82 Greene, 2005a; see also 2005b, p. 59; 2008, p. 43; Greene et al., 2004, pp. 389–390; Singer,
2005, pp. 333–337.
83 Greene et al., 2004, pp. 389–390.
84 Altruistic punishment has been suggested to have evolved through group selection (Bowles
and Gintis, 2004; Boyd et al., 2003, see also Sober and Wilson, 1999). Others have suggested that
retributive behavior was adaptive because it confers reputational benefits on the punisher (Barclay, 2006; Kurzban et al., 2007, see also Gintis et al., 2001). On these two alternative explanations of punishment, refer to Buss, 2014, p. 294. On the evolution of incest aversion, see Lieberman et al., 2003.

moral dispositions evolved, and it is no surprise that these dispositions are implemented emotionally.[85]

This is in line with other dual-process accounts, which typically associate emotional processing with the evolutionarily old quick and automatic subsystem.[86] Evidence of the emotional nature of deontological responses is therefore treated as evidence of their evolutionary background. This is how dual-process theory and the underlying neuroscientific evidence support the argument from evolutionary history. It is worth noting, though, that the 'emotional' nature of a moral response is arguably neither a necessary nor a sufficient indicator of its being the product of evolution. While dual-process theory provides some evidence of the evolutionary hypothesis, the strength of this evidence should not be overstated.

2.4 The backfiring problem

As a debunking argument, the thrust of Greene and Singer's empirically informed attack on deontology is in the first instance negative. If successful, it defeats intuitions and arguments in support of deontology. It does not provide any positive support for utilitarianism. But the dialectical aim of the project is not just to refute deontology but to vindicate utilitarianism. The idea is that if all intuitions and arguments in defense of deontology have been debunked, we are left only with evidence in support of utilitarianism, and this tilts the balance of evidence in favor of utilitarianism. This strategy of vindicating utilitarianism, however, presupposes that the evidence in support of utilitarianism does not itself fall prey to a similar debunking argument. If it can be shown that utilitarianism is debunkable, too, this would do little to salvage deontology. But it would turn the success of the debunking argument into a pyrrhic victory. The debunking argument might still be philosophically interesting in its own right. It would establish that deontological theories lack justification. But it would fail to achieve the dialectical aim of establishing utilitarianism in its stead. This, I submit, is precisely why the argument from evolutionary history fails.[87] Like the other de-

---

85 Greene, 2008, p. 60.
86 See e.g. Evans, 2008, pp. 256–257; Kahneman, 2003, p. 698.
87 Versions of the backfiring problem are discussed in Berker, 2009, pp. 319–320; Kahane, 2014a; Mason, 2011, pp. 452–455; Rini, 2016; Sauer, 2018, pp. 89–90; Tersman, 2008, pp. 400–403; Vavova, 2014, pp. 93–95.

bunking programs examined in this book, it backfires, and no plausible way of defusing the backfiring problem has been offered.

There are, in principle, two ways in which utilitarians may attempt to dispel concerns that utilitarianism, too, is susceptible to some debunking argument or other. First, they may dispute that utilitarianism is even based on intuitions in the first place. While deontology is essentially emotional and intuitive, utilitarianism is 'cognitive' and non-intuitive, or so they might argue. And if utilitarianism is not based on intuitions to begin with, debunking arguments that aim at defeating the evidential force of intuitions are an unsuitable means of challenging utilitarianism. Second, they might concede that utilitarianism rests on intuitions, too, but only to insist that there is no plausible debunking explanation of these intuitions. The mere in-principle *possibility* of there being a debunking explanation of utilitarianism need not worry utilitarians too much. What matters is whether a compelling debunking explanation can actually be provided or not. And utilitarians might argue that the central tenets of utilitarianism are not amenable to a plausible debunking explanation.

At times, Singer seems drawn to the former view, that is, to the claim that utilitarianism can do without intuitions altogether. He suggests "taking a critical stance toward common intuitions", and he has dismissed "the view that we must test our normative theories against our intuitions" as "evidently erroneous".[88] The notion, however, that utilitarianism does not rely on intuitions is implausible. To be sure, utilitarians have suggested that we give less credit to intuitions about specific cases, such as about the permissibility of pushing a person in front of a trolley or about our obligation to donate money to starving people in faraway countries. But utilitarians do of course affirm principles of a more general kind, such as that every person's wellbeing matters the same and that pain or the frustration of preferences are bad. And the affirmation of these more general principles *is* based on intuitions. Indeed, the very reason why utilitarians think that we should be skeptical about our responses to specific cases is precisely that these responses have turned out to clash with intuitions of a more general kind. For instance, one reason why we should distrust our intuition that we have only a weak obligation to help starving people in remote countries is that we have the more general intuition that we have an obligation to mitigate human suffering if we can do so without significant costs to ourselves. It would therefore be misleading to claim that utilitarians need not invoke intuitions.[89]

---

88 Singer, 2005, p. 332 and Singer, 1999, p. 316, respectively.
89 Similarly Huemer, 2009, pp. 371–376.

The second strategy appears more promising, and it is also the strategy that Singer has eventually opted for (while Greene hast mostly abandoned the argument from evolutionary history, apparently in response to the backfiring problem). Instead of denying that utilitarianism is based on intuitions, he argues that these intuitions resist the kind of genealogical debunking explanations that undermine deontology. Singer alleges that these intuitions are not the "outcome of our evolutionary past."[90] This is a more interesting proposal, which deserves to be considered in somewhat greater detail.

Together with Katarzyna de Lazari-Radek, Singer has argued that the central axiom of utilitarianism – what Henry Sidgwick calls the principle of universal benevolence – is not plausibly debunkable.[91] Sidgwick's principle of universal benevolence states that "each one is morally bound to regard the good of any other individual as much as his own, except in so far as he judges it to be less, when impartially viewed, or less certainly knowable or attainable by him."[92] The principle captures the kind of impartiality that is essential to utilitarianism and that distinguishes utilitarianism from many deontological theories. Singer and de Lazari-Radek take it that belief in this principle is not plausibly explainable in evolutionary terms. There are evolutionary explanations of how altruistic behavior may have evolved (as we shall later see in more detail). But the kind of altruism that can be explained in evolutionary terms is rather limited in scope. We can explain altruism towards kin, friends and maybe members of one's own group. But the notion that complete strangers are on the same moral footing as people close to us runs counter to the logic of evolution. De Lazari-Radek and Singer claim, convincingly, that it is "difficult to see any evolutionary forces that could have favored universal altruism of the sort that is required by the axiom of rational benevolence. On the contrary, there are strong evolutionary forces that would tend to eliminate it."[93] What is more, they point out that a principle along the lines of the principle of universal benevolence has come to be endorsed independently by different cultures.[94] This supports their conjecture that this principle strikes us as plausible quite simply because it is supported by reason rather than the result of historical or cultural accident.[95] Of course, de Lazari-Radek and Singer's argument fails to prove that the principle of univer-

---

90 Singer, 2005, p. 350.

91 de Lazari-Radek and Singer, 2012, 2014.

92 Sidgwick, 1981, book III, ch. XIII.

93 de Lazari-Radek and Singer, 2012, p. 19.

94 de Lazari-Radek and Singer, 2012, pp. 25–26.

95 This might cast doubt on Tersman's suggested debunking explanation of this principle (Tersman, 2008, pp. 401–402).

sal benevolence is in principle un-debunkable. But the burden of proof rests on the would-be debunker of utilitarianism.[96]

However, even if de Lazari-Radek and Singer's reasoning is sound, utilitarianism is not yet off the hook. There is another component of utilitarianism that is vulnerable to a debunking challenge, a component that the above argument fails to protect. Even if the principle that the wellbeing of all people counts the same should resist debunking attempts, we still need a substantial conception of what these people's wellbeing actually consists in. And theories about what their wellbeing consists in can be debunked, too. Indeed, as Guy Kahane has observed, the two classic utilitarian suggestions for what is good for a person appear to be readily amenable to debunking explanations:

> Our evaluative beliefs about pain and pleasure are perhaps the easiest to explain in evolutionary terms. It will be hard, at best, to find a serious evolutionary theorist who would deny this. These hedonic beliefs fall at one end of the scale, with beliefs about the value of fulfilling our desires probably coming a fairly close second.[97]

This means that appeals to evolutionary considerations are unlikely to establish anything resembling traditional utilitarianism, which recommends the maximization of pleasure or preference-fulfilment. Indeed, both Singer and Greene advocate versions hedonistic utilitarianism (although Singer used to favor preference utilitarianism).[98]

De Lazari-Radek and Singer have offered a twofold response to this problem. Their first argument is that we cannot be mistaken about the badness of pain and the goodness of pleasure because "[p]ain and pleasure are states of consciousness and we have direct knowledge of them. How could knowing something about the origins of these states undermine our judgment that, considered just as a state of consciousness, they are good of bad?"[99]

To illustrate this point, they invite us to imagine an experiment in which, through hypnosis, the participants are made to have a headache when they encounter a specific cue (e. g. the word 'often'). The participants would presumably state that the headache they experienced during this experiment is 'bad'. But

---

96 For two attempts to discharge this burden, see Andes, 2019; Tersman, 2008.

97 Kahane, 2014a, p. 334. Similarly, Street writes "it is of course no mystery whatsoever, from an evolutionary point of view, why we and other animals came to take the sensations associated with bodily [harm] to count in favor of what would avoid, lessen, or stop them rather than in favor of what would bring about and intensify them." (2006, p. 150)

98 See de Lazari-Radek and Singer, 2014, p. xviii; Greene, 2013, pp. 157–161; Singer and de Lazari-Radek, 2016. Singer espouses preference utilitarianism in Singer, 1993.

99 de Lazari-Radek and Singer, 2014, p. 267.

would they recant their judgment that they had a bad experience once they are debriefed and learn that they experienced this headache as the result of hypnosis?

> Presumably not. Nothing they learned about the origins of the experience they had just had would be grounds for altering their judgment of how bad it felt at the time, because that is something of which they had direct acquaintance. Pain that is the result of an illusion is no less bad than pain that is the result of something real, and pain that is the result of evolutionary selection is no less bad than pain that has other origins, whatever they might be.[100]

But this response is confused. It confuses explanations of why we are in a state of pain and explanations of why we believe that pain is bad. It may be true that no explanation of the former type can undermine the justification of the participants' belief that they were really in a state of pain. Maybe people cannot be mistaken about whether they are in a state of pain or not, whatever the origins of this pain may be. But the evolutionary debunking argument does not seek to provide an explanation of why people feel pain, or of what pain is the 'result' of. Rather, it seeks to provide an explanation of the latter type, that is, an explanation of why people judge that pain is bad. Thought experiments about whether people would, or ought to, recant their judgment that they felt pain upon learning about the origins of this pain are beside the point. De Lazari-Radek's and Singer's first response misses the point and fails to defuse the challenge.[101]

Their second response is that it is not necessary to believe that pain is bad and pleasure good in order to be motivated to avoid pain and to seek pleasure. For pain and pleasure are intrinsically motivating. There is no need for additional normative beliefs to this effect in order for our ancestors to show adaptive behavior.[102] While this is true, the argument overlooks that having these normative beliefs would probably be adaptive by making the adaptive behavior even *more likely.* The fact that the way pleasure and pain feel already has a motivating effect does not mean that additional motivation would not be adaptive. Note that there are other plausible cases of 'moral overdetermination'. Many of the moral beliefs that are good candidates for evolutionary explanations motivate people to perform actions that they are naturally motivated to perform anyway. For example, a good candidate for an evolutionary explanation is the belief that we ought to help people in need who are close to us. But typically, we also naturally *enjoy* helping these people. Likewise, the belief that we have a greater obligation to-

---

100 de Lazari-Radek and Singer, 2014, p. 268.
101 See also Street's comments on the badness of pain (2006, pp. 144–152).
102 de Lazari-Radek and Singer, 2014, pp. 268–289; similarly Bramble, 2017, p. 97; Jaquet, 2018.

wards our own children than towards strangers seems readily explainable in evolutionary terms. But we also *love* our own children more than strangers, which is why we naturally tend to look after and support the former more than the latter. It is plausible that we have acquired these moral beliefs because they provided a useful *additional* incentive to perform the evolutionarily adaptive action.

What is more, de Lazari-Radek and Singer focus exclusively on the egocentric perspective. But humans are cooperative creatures who often seek to make *others'* lives go well. And it is plausible to assume that they evolved to believe that *others'* wellbeing is reduced by pain and increased by pleasure. For instance, given that pain is correlated with injury and injury is correlated with reduced reproductive success, the belief that pain is bad for one's kin tends to increase one's inclusive fitness and may thus have been adaptive. The fact that people (e.g. one's kin) are already motivated to avoid pain is not relevant once we assume this allocentric perspective.

It is not promising to switch to preference utilitarianism instead, that is, to espouse a preference-based account of wellbeing. In order to come up with a promising evolutionary debunking explanation of such preference-based views, we need not even insist that it can be adaptive to have an additional incentive (or to adopt the allocentric perspective). Most subjectivists defend an idealizing version of subjectivism, according to which what is good for a person is a function of the preferences (or desires, pro-attitudes, etc.) she would have under suitably idealized circumstances.[103] The purpose of this idealization is to filter out preferences that are irrational, ill-informed or that reflect some other error or bias, and to thus make sure that subjectivism is extensionally adequate. As a result, what is good for a person does often not coincide with what she *actually* prefers, that is, with what she prefers in her pre-idealized state. This means that an evolutionary debunking explanation of subjectivism about wellbeing cannot be dismissed on the grounds that people would be automatically motivated to seek what is good for them, anyway. This would only be true for non-idealized versions of subjectivism, which few subjectivists (or utilitarians, for that matter) accept.

And indeed, an evolutionary explanation of why one might think that wellbeing is a function of idealized preferences is anything but far-fetched. Evolution has equipped living organisms such as humans and many animals with preferences or desires that by and large lead to behavior that increase their fitness. But sometimes they do not. From an evolutionary point of view, it is arguably better to act on one's suitably idealized preferences than to always act on one's actual

---

103 See e.g. Brandt, 1979; Railton, 1986; Rosati, 1996.

preferences, especially in a complex and changing environment. For example, it is better to eat what one would desire to eat if one had all information about the food item and the consequences of eating it, than to simply always eat what one actually desires to eat. The belief that one should act on one's idealized preferences encourages one to step back from one's actual preferences and to consider whether they might be defective in a way that would decrease wellbeing if acted upon. A belief of this sort may very well have been adaptive.[104]

To conclude, it is doubtful that evolutionary considerations support utilitarianism in the way Greene, Singer and, more recently, de Lazari-Radek imagine. It may be true that the principle of universal benevolence is not susceptible to an evolutionary debunking argument. But utilitarian debunkers must also put forth some account of personal welfare, and – pace de Lazari-Radek and Singer — the go-to accounts of personal welfare *do* seem susceptible to debunking.[105] This does not vitiate Greene and Singer's efforts to debunk deontological intuitions, but it means that they will fail to achieve the dialectical aim of vindicating utilitarianism.

2.5 The scope problem

The argument from evolutionary history backfires. But not only does it backfire. With respect to many deontological views, it does not fire at all, so to speak. Consider that the argument from evolutionary history rests pivotally on the genealogical claim that our deontological intuitions are remnants of our evolutionary past. They must be jettisoned because of their dubious genealogy. While the hypothesis that deontological intuitions are residues of our evolutionary past is certainly not implausible, evidence for this has only been offered for intuitions about sacrificial dilemmas, punishment, our obligation to help, and incest.

---

104 The subjectivist move has been explored and defended by Jaquet (2018) and Rowland (2019). But in a way, they themselves provide the reason why the belief in idealizing subjectivism may be amenable to an evolutionary explanation. Jaquet observes correctly that "from the evolutionary standpoint, not all our first order desires should be satisfied." (2018, p. 1158; see also Rowland, 2019, p. 185) He cites this observation as a reason why the belief in non-idealizing subjectivism is not a plausible candidate for an evolutionary explanation. Whether this is true or not, the same observation is a reason why *idealizing* subjectivism *is* a plausible candidate for an evolutionary explanation. And preference utilitarians usually opt for the idealized approach.
105 In fact, not only hedonistic and preference-fulfilment accounts are vulnerable to debunking. Many other widely-held beliefs about what is good for a person – friendship and community, having children, knowledge, etc. – are suitable targets for evolutionary debunking arguments, too.

But, as others have noted before, these are but a small selection from an enormous range of ethical problems that one can have deontological intuitions about. Other questions concern, for instance, lying, promising, distributive justice, property rights, the authority of law, the treatment of animals and the environment, and so on.[106] Many deontological intuitions about questions related to these issues are not affected by Greene and Singer's fairly circumscribed attack on deontological intuitions. Thus, even if Greene and Singer should have successfully shown that *some* deontological intuitions can be explained away in evolutionary terms, this is still a far cry from showing that deontological intuitions are unreliable as a class, or, in Greene's words, that deontology "as a school of normative moral thought" should be called into question.[107]

But the situation is worse than that. Greene and Singer's findings seem to be incomplete even with regard to sacrificial dilemmas, even though their argument focuses on sacrificial dilemmas. Greene and Singer suggest that our responses to sacrificial dilemmas vary as a function of whether they are 'up close and personal' or not, and, on this basis, they suggest an evolutionary explanation of why we respond to the 'personalness' of a dilemma. However, while it may be true that 'up close and personal' violations trigger deontological intuitions, it is easy to think of impersonal dilemmas that trigger deontological intuitions, too.

Consider the following three scenarios, all of which feature the unfortunate heavy person:

Rifle
A heavy person is standing on the footbridge and could block the trolley that is headed for the five workers on the track. Unlike in *Footbridge*, you are too weak to push the person off the bridge onto the tracks below. The heavy person would wrestle you down. Fortunately, you happen to carry a rifle with you, as you were on your way to a hunting trip. If you aim for the heavy person's head (from a distance of, say, 10 meters), this will kill him and make him fall onto the tracks below, thus blocking the trolley and saving the five workers.[108]

Hypnosis
A heavy person is standing on the footbridge and could block the trolley that is headed for the five workers on the track. Unlike in *Footbridge*, you are too weak to push the person off the bridge onto the tracks below. The heavy person would wrestle you down. Fortunately,

---

106 As Berker observes: "To claim that characteristically deontological judgments only concern bodily harms is nothing short of preposterous; after all, the stock in trade of deontology is supposed to involve not just prohibitions on murder and mayhem, but also requirements against lying, promise breaking, coercion, and the like." (2009, p. 311; see also Dean, 2010, p. 48; Kahane, 2012, pp. 521–522; 2014b, p. 13; Kahane et al., 2012; Mason, 2011, p. 444).
107 Greene, 2008, p. 36.
108 On trolley dilemmas involving projectiles, see Greene, 2013, p. 378; 2016, p. 177.

you are a skilled hypnotizer. You can hypnotize the heavy person and make him jump onto the tracks below, which would kill him but block the trolley and save the five workers.

Electroshock
A heavy person, who could block the trolley headed for the five workers, is about to cross the tracks at a location between the trolley and the five workers. By hitting a button, you can send electroshocks through the rails and electrocute the heavy person the moment he crosses the tracks. The five workers are too far down the track to receive any electric shocks. Hitting the button will instantly kill the heavy person, and his body will block the trolley, saving the five workers.

Each of these three scenarios seems to elicit a deontological intuition. Intuitively, it seems abhorrent to sacrifice the heavy person in each of the three situations. But none of these dilemmas involve 'up close and personal' violations. None of them involve the sort of violation that played a role in our ancestral environment and that 'a chimp can understand'.[109] Surely, our ancestors did not kill each other using rifles, hypnosis or electroshocks (nor, for that matter, do chimps). It is not clear, from an evolutionary point of view, why these dilemmas should trigger deontological intuitions.[110] By implication, these deontological responses cannot easily be debunked as products of evolution, either, at least not in any obvious way. It may be true that *some* deontological responses to sacrificial dilemmas can be explained away in evolutionary terms. But it is easy to come up with sacrificial dilemmas that elicit deontological responses and that do not fit the evolutionary narrative. To be sure, it is possible that there is an evolutionary (or some other) debunking explanation of our deontological responses to these scenarios, too. But so far, no such explanation has been provided, and the burden of proof is on Greene and Singer. Until such an explanation has been offered, their debunking of deontological intuitions in sacrificial dilemmas remains very incomplete.[111]

---

109 Examples like these can easily be multiplied. Berker mentions other counterexamples, which do not, however, involve means that were not available to our Pleistocene ancestors (2009, p. 323 n73).

110 Admittedly, these dilemmas might qualify as 'up close and personal' according to how this variable was initially operationalized in the 2001 study. But this is only because 'up close and personal' was operationalized in a questionable manner (Berker, 2009, p. 312). What ultimately matters is whether they involve the sort of violence that was present in our ancestral environment.

111 It is true that in each of these dilemmas the victim is used as a means to an end. As we shall see further below, Greene has also proposed an evolutionary debunking explanation of why we treat intended harm differently from foreseen harm. But it is doubtful that this factor alone explains our deontological intuitions about these three scenarios. The means/end factor

The set of debunked deontological intuitions is thus rather small. While the proposed evolutionary debunking explanations may be correct, they affect only a small subset of our deontological intuitions. Indeed, they even fail to debunk many of our deontological intuitions specifically about sacrificial dilemmas. As we shall see later, this also reduces the force of the argument from confabulation. To be sure, the limited scope of the argument does not salvage the targeted deontological intuitions. But it does put the force of Greene and Singer's challenge into perspective. On the whole, the argument from evolutionary history is not only too destructive, offering a method that can also be used against utilitarian judgments, but at the same time too weak and narrow to pose much of a threat to deontology.

---

on its own (without the factor of personal force) has, as Greene notes, at best a relatively weak effect (Greene, 2013, pp. 218–222; 2016, p. 177; Greene et al., 2009, p. 369).

3 Deontology, Utilitarianism, and Experimental Ethics

3.1 Introduction

Unlike the argument from evolutionary history and the to-be-considered functionalist argument, the argument from moral irrelevance does not rely on evolutionary hypotheses about the origins of moral judgments. Indeed, as will be discussed in more detail below, it does not even seem to rely on dual-process theory. Instead, it invokes experimental findings about which factors of a moral scenario people's moral intuitions are triggered by.

In Greene and colleagues' initial 2001 study, a dilemma was classified as 'up close and personal' – and thus as likely to elicit a deontological response – if it met the following three criteria: "the action in question (a) could reasonably be expected to lead to serious bodily harm (b) to a particular person or a member or members of a particular group of people (c) where this harm is not the result of deflecting an existing threat."[112] All other moral dilemmas were classified as 'impersonal'. This initial operationalization was acknowledged to be imperfect and provisional. It was a rough guess, which was made in order to test the dual-process hypothesis.[113] In a later study, Greene and colleagues updated this provisional proposal by experimentally testing people's responses to different variations of the trolley dilemmas. The argument from moral irrelevance is primarily based on the findings from this study.

Greene and colleagues investigated the impact of two variables in particular: First, they manipulated whether harm was inflicted intentionally as a means to an end (as in *Loop*) or as an unintended, merely foreseen side-effect (as in *Switch*). Second, they manipulated whether harm was inflicted through the use of what they call 'personal force' or not. Harm is inflicted by means of personal force "when the force that directly impacts the other is generated by the agent's muscles, as when one pushes another with one's hands or with a rigid object."[114] An example of a scenario that involves personal force is *Footbridge*, while *Loop*

---

112 Greene et al., 2001, p. 2107.

113 Greene et al., 2001, p. 2107; see also 2009; 2010, p. 27; 2014, p. 701 n17. Note that they did not classify dilemmas by simply testing whether they tend to elicit deontological or consequentialist responses.

114 Greene et al., 2009, p. 365.

https://doi.org/10.1515/9783110750195-004

and *Switch* are scenarios that do not involve personal force.[115] Both of these factors – intention and personal force – had previously been discussed in the literature as possible candidates for the feature that determines people's intuitions.[116] Greene and colleagues tested specifically whether it might be the *conjunction* of these two factors that determines whether a scenario elicits a deontological or utilitarian response.[117] They instructed their participants to respond to four different types of dilemmas, which exhibited either one, both or neither of these two features. It was found that it was indeed the combination of intention and personal force that was most likely to elicit deontological responses, while each of these features on their own had no or little effect.[118] It is thus the conjunction of intention and personal force that Greene considers to be the decisive factor that renders a dilemma 'personal' in the relevant sense and that makes it trigger deontological responses.[119]

A related unpublished experimental study invoked by Greene concerns people's sensitivity to spatial distance. The study, which was inspired by Singer's drowning child scenario, suggests that people's sense of moral obligation towards people in need varies depending upon spatial distance. Mere spatial distance determines the extent to which we feel morally obliged to, for instance, rescue a dying child.[120]

The argument from moral irrelevance asserts that we should dismiss deontological intuitions on the grounds that they have been found, or will be found, to be responsive to factors that lack moral significance, such as personal force and spatial distance. An observation made by Greene nicely captures the idea of identifying morally irrelevant factors: "Were a friend to call you from a set of trolley tracks seeking moral advice, you would probably not say, 'Well, that depends. Would you have to push the guy, or could you do it with a switch?'"[121]

---

115 The concept of personal force integrates the earlier assumption that the infliction of harm is judged to be permissible when an existing threat is merely deflected.
116 Greene, 2009, p. 365.
117 The study offers a solution to the descriptive part of the trolley problem (which principles govern our responses to trolley scenarios?), not to its moral part (which responses are correct?).
118 This finding was further supported by a reanalysis of data from a study by Fiery Cushman and colleagues, which had also tested people's responses to dilemmas of these four different types (Cushman et al., 2006).
119 In some places, he has suggested that our responses are also sensitive to the difference between doing and allowing. This distinction is closely related to personal force, because omissions cannot possibly involve the use of personal force (Greene, 2013, p. 247).
120 Musen and Greene, MS; Singer, 1972.
121 Greene, 2016, p. 176.

The same test can be used for any other factor the relevance of which we would like to determine.

This chapter argues that deontologists need not be too concerned about the attempt to debunk deontology by showing deontological intuitions to be responsive to morally irrelevant factors. It also offers some more general lessons about the structure and philosophical value of arguments from moral irrelevance (anti-deontological and other), and about the significance of experimental ethics. I begin with a more detailed analysis of the structure of the argument from moral irrelevance, before exploring how, again due to the backfiring problem and the scope problem, the argument fails to put pressure on deontology. I close with some reflections on the value of experimental ethics.

3.2 The argument from moral irrelevance

Normally, when we have different intuitions about similar moral cases, we take this to indicate that there is a moral difference between these cases. This is because we take our intuitions to have responded to a morally relevant difference. But if it turns out that our case-specific intuitions are responding to a factor that lacks moral significance, we no longer have reason to trust our case-specific intuitions that suggest that there is a moral difference. This is the basic logic behind arguments from moral irrelevance.

Two different types of moral intuitions play a role in arguments from moral irrelevance. The target of such arguments are case-specific intuitions, that is, intuitions about what is the right thing to do in a concrete case. Greene's argument, for instance, targets our case-specific deontological intuitions in the footbridge case. But they also rely on an intuition about a moral principle at a higher level of generality, namely on an intuition about whether a given feature of a scenario matters from a moral point of view. Greene's argument rests on the intuition that the involvement of personal force in a trolley scenario does not matter from a moral point of view. An intuition of this sort does not, on its own, tell us what to do in a concrete case, but it tells us whether two cases, e. g. *Switch* and *Footbridge*, should be treated differently due to the presence or absence of this feature.[122]

Greene's argument from moral irrelevance can be formalized as follows:

---

[122] The distinction between these two types of intuitions is common in the literature, see e.g. Greene, 2014, p. 724; Kagan, 1998, pp. 13–14; Kamm, 1993, pp. 5–7; McMahan, 2013; Sandberg and Juth, 2011, p. 213

The Argument from Moral Irrelevance

P1. Empirical evidence suggests that we have different (utilitarian vs. deontological) case-specific intuitions about similar moral cases due to the presence or absence of personal force.

P2. Personal force is morally irrelevant.

C1. We have different case-specific intuitions (utilitarian vs. deontological) about similar moral cases due to the presence or absence of a morally irrelevant factor.

P3. If we have different case-specific intuitions (utilitarian vs. deontological) about similar moral cases due to the presence or absence of a morally irrelevant factor, these intuitions cannot both be sound.

C2. The utilitarian intuition and the deontological intuition cannot both be sound.

P4. The utilitarian intuition is sound.

C3. The deontological intuition is not sound.

The experimental finding that our case-specific intuitions are responsive to personal force is contained in premise 1. Premise 2 is a conventional normative premise stating that this factor is morally insignificant. This premise rests on a general, rather than case-specific, intuition about which properties matter from a moral point of view. Premise 3 states the core idea behind arguments from moral irrelevance explained above. We usually regard our having different case-specific intuitions about similar moral cases as showing that these cases differ morally, because we assume that our case-specific intuitions are responding to such a morally relevant difference. But if we learn that our case-specific intuitions are responsive to a morally irrelevant factor, which does not justify having different case-specific intuitions, there must be something wrong with one of these case-specific intuitions. This is a symmetrical finding, as it were. It does not yet entail that the deontological response ("It is impermissible to shove the person off the footbridge.") rather than the consequentialist one ("It is permissible to hit the switch.") is flawed. At this stage, we can only draw the preliminary conclusion C2 that one of the two intuitions should be dismissed.[123]

But Greene seems to take it that our consequentialist case-specific intuitions in scenarios without personal force – that it is permissible to hit the switch – can be assumed to be correct (P4). The consequentialist judgment about scenarios

---

123 As previously observed by Kumar and Campbell, 2012, pp. 317–218; see also Kumar and May, 2019; May, 2018, pp. 113–115.

without personal force is regarded as a moral fixed-point, so to speak.[124] Given then that personal force is not a morally relevant consideration, the deontological case-specific intuition in personal dilemmas must be erroneous. The deontological case-specific intuition does not give us reason to move away from the consequentialist default. Greene claims "that once all of the inner workings of our judgments are revealed by science, there will be nothing left for deontologists. All of the factors that *push us away from consequentialism* will, once brought into the light, turn out to be things that we will all regard as morally irrelevant."[125] That is, he treats consequentialist case-specific responses as the moral default any deviation from which needs to be justified. This premise allows him to draw conclusion C3, which states that the deontological case-specific intuition in the *Footbridge* case is the culprit.[126] The same type of argument is used by Greene to challenge the deontological case-specific intuition that it is morally acceptable to let faraway children starve by not donating to charity.

Arguments from moral irrelevance are 'liberationist' in spirit. They suggest that we should discount many of our case-specific intuitions. The liberationist approach contrasts with the 'preservationist' approach, which seeks to preserve our case-specific intuitions. Peter Unger, who coined these terms and who is himself a chief proponent of liberationism, explains:

> On [the] *Liberationist* view, folks' intuitive moral responses to many specific cases derive from sources far removed from our Values and, so, they fail to reflect the Values, often even pointing in the opposite direction. So even as the Perservationist seeks (almost) always to *preserve* the appearances promoted by these responses, the Liberationist seeks often to *liberate* us from such appearances.[127]

A general intuition about which properties are morally relevant (P2) is invoked in an attempt to undermine case-specific intuitions. To be sure, Greene ultimately seeks to refute deontology as a general theory. But he proceeds by debunking case-specific deontological intuitions such as the above rather than deontological principles at a higher level of generality.

---

124 At one point, Greene seems reluctant to explicitly endorse this assumption (2014, p. 713), but he *has* to if the argument is to challenge the deontological intuition. Due to the mentioned symmetry, he cannot attack the deontological intuition directly by claiming that it, but not the consequentialist response, is triggered by the irrelevant factor.

125 Greene, 2010, p. 21, my emphasis.

126 I am here expanding and, I hope, improving on previous characterizations of this type argument (Berker, 2009, p. 321; Kumar and Campbell, 2012; Sauer, 2018, p. 43).

127 Unger, 1997, pp. 11–12.

The general idea behind arguments from moral irrelevance is not new. Singer's suggestion that there is no morally relevant difference between a starving child in a remote country and a nearby drowning child as well as Unger's book-length elaboration of Singer's insight are two notable applications of this approach.[128] Greene's reasoning is clearly inspired by their work. But the current revival of this approach is different in that it is driven by experimental investigations into which factors trigger our responses. Earlier such arguments were armchair-based.[129] Regina Rini, another advocate of this approach, asserts that the primary use of experimental moral psychology for normative moral theory is precisely that of informing such arguments from moral irrelevance: "[E]mpirical investigation allows us to identify psychological factors that influence our moral judgments, yet which we do not reflectively regard as surviving normative abstraction."[130]

3.3 The backfiring problem

Arguments from moral irrelevance can be made to work. But their usefulness for the utilitarian project is very limited, chiefly because utilitarian would-be debunkers face the backfiring problem all over again. While arguments from moral irrelevance may be used to undermine some deontological case-specific intuitions, they may just as well turn out to undermine utilitarian responses. This time around, the backfiring problem appears in three different guises.

First, the method may backfire by undermining the intuition about which factors are morally relevant rather than the deontological case-specific intuition. Consider that any tension between moral intuitions at different levels of generality can be resolved in more than just one way. Greene assumes that in light of such a clash of intuitions, we should dismiss the case-specific deontological intuition, which clashes with the more general intuition about the irrelevance of some factor and the case-specific consequentialist one. In many cases of a conflict of intuitions, this may well be the reasonable thing to do. In other situations, however, it seems more reasonable to jettison our general judgment about the

---

128 Singer, 1972; Unger, 1997.

129 Unger has, however, "[i]nformally and intermittently [...] asked many students, colleagues and friends" for their intuitions (1997, p 31).

130 Rini, 2013, p. 267. The morally irrelevant factors that Rini discusses also include factors that are external to the moral scenarios themselves, such as framing effects and psychological manipulation. I return to this point below. Elsewhere, Rini has highlighted problems with selective debunking arguments based on such empirical evidence (2016).

irrelevance of this factor given that our case-specific intuitions are responsive to it. Applied to the case at hand, it means that deontologists could retort that the fact that our responses are sensitive to personal force just goes to show that personal force *is* a morally relevant factor.[131] Rather than to conclude that one of the case-specific intuitions must be wrong (C2), we may have to reconsider P2, that is, our assumption about the irrelevance of the factor to which our intuitions are responsive to.

To see this more clearly, note that something needs to be said about the relationship between intuitions at different levels of generality and about how to resolve conflicts between them. The most natural view on this matter is that how much confidence we should have in case-specific and general intuitions is simply a function of the intrinsic strengths of these intuitions. As ethical intuitionist Huemer explains, "[s]ome appearances are stronger than others – as we say, some things are 'more obvious' than others – and this determines what we hold on to and what we reject in case of a conflict."[132] Which intuitions we should trust would depend primarily on their strengths, not their level of generality, and the way to adjudicate a conflict would be to attend to the relative strengths of these intuitions. We must then decide on a case-by-case basis which way the tension between case-specific intuitions and general intuitions is to be resolved. In some cases, particularly strong general intuitions may prompt us to dismiss conflicting case-specific intuitions. In other cases, case-specific intuitions may be so compelling as to require a revision of more general principles. What matters, then, is how compelling or 'obvious' the individual intuitions are, not their level of generality as such. This is a plausible method of moral theory construction, which a significant portion of ethicists are explicitly or implicitly committed to. It is also in line with the method of reflective equilibrium, which takes seriously judgments at different levels of abstraction and allows that judgments of both types may have to be revised in light of the others.[133]

---

131 See Bruni et al., 2014, p. 170; Ernst, 2007, p. 136; Kamm, 2007, p. 417.

132 Huemer, 2005, p. 100; see also DePaul, 2006, pp. 599–600. Huemer points out elsewhere, however, that case-specific intuitions may eventually turn out to be more susceptible to debunking explanations (2008, p. 383).

133 In fact, even Kamm, the leader of the preservationist camp, acknowledges, if only by lip-service, that a moral principle derived from case-specific intuitions may stand in need of further validation: We must "consider the principle on its own, to see if it expresses some plausible value or conception of the person or relations between persons. This is necessary to justify it as a *correct* principle, one that has normative weight, not merely one that makes all of the case judgments cohere." (2007, p. 5, see also pp. 346, 379). In practice, Kamm shows relatively little interest in whether a principle considered on its own is plausible (Nye, 2015, p. 627).

This methodological assumption does not imply that one cannot demonstrate that *some* intuitively compelling case-specific deontological intuitions must be relinquished as they clash with even more compelling intuitions at a higher level of generality and plausible consequentialist judgments. Perhaps, the intuition that personal force is morally irrelevant and the judgment that it is permissible to hit the switch in *Switch* are really so compelling as to overrule the intuition that it is impermissible to shove the person off the bridge, rather than the other way round.[134] Whether this particular argument succeeds or not is not my principal concern here. Rather, my concern is whether this approach can be used to systematically debunk deontological case-specific intuitions on a large scale. And the above methodological assumption implies that this is unlikely. For it means that Greene's method of debunking deontology does not scale well. Even granting that his debunking argument against deontological intuitions that are responsive to personal force and spatial distance succeeds, it would be a surprise if all or even the bulk of case-specific deontological intuitions can eventually be undermined in this way. Instead, it is to be expected that there are many strong deontological case-specific intuitions that will force us to reconsider the general principles with which they clash, rather than vice versa. Deontological cases-specific intuitions can themselves be important moral data points, which more general moral principles must accommodate.

When a debunking attempt fails in this manner, it does not just mean that the deontological case-specific intuition withstands the debunking attempt. The debunking attempt genuinely *backfires* in that it undermines the utilitarian general intuition on which it is based. The utilitarian would-be debunker relies on a judgment about the moral irrelevance of some factor (e.g. personal force) that is best described as utilitarian. It is utilitarian in that it is in line with the utilitarian tenet that no factors are morally relevant other than those that are relevant for the maximization of wellbeing. But if the deontological case-specific intuition is so compelling that it requires a revision of this general intuition, this effectively means that the utilitarian would-be debunker ends up having to accept that factors other than those that are relevant for the maximization of wellbeing (e.g. personal force) *are* morally relevant, contrary to what utilitarianism suggests.

In light of this problem, utilitarian debunkers might maintain that there is some principled rationale for why we should always give priority to general intuitions over case-specific ones, whatever this rationale might be. According to

---

134 I am here bracketing the problem that intention *does* seem to be a morally relevant factor. I return to this problem below.

this view, case-specific intuitions can, as a rule, be assumed to be significantly less reliable than general intuitions, or indeed completely unreliable. Whenever there is a clash between case-specific intuitions and a general intuition, it is always the latter that prevails, even when the former are intuitively compelling.[135]

Howard Nye, for instance, contends that case-specific intuitions have no justificatory force at all, only the ancillary function of clarifying and illustrating more general principles.[136] Distrust towards case-specific intuitions is also common among utilitarian thinkers. Singer seems to endorse the priority of general judgments in his famous *Famine, Affluence, and Morality*. People's case-specific verdicts militate against his view that indifference towards the plight of people in remote countries is morally unacceptable. But "the way people do in fact judge has nothing to do with the validity of my conclusion. My conclusion follows from the principle which I advanced earlier, and unless that principle is rejected, or the arguments shown to be unsound, I think the conclusion must stand, however strange it appears."[137] Unger's development of Singer's argument is also informed by the liberationist view that general judgments should correct our case-specific judgments, rather than vice versa.[138] Building upon this tradition, Greene and others who wish to advance arguments from moral irrelevance could maintain that intuitions at a higher level of generality should be taken to be more reliable than case-specific ones *as a matter of principle*, whatever the rationale behind this principle might be.

---

135 A third possibility is to assert that case-specific intuitions have priority over general ones. Preservationists like Frances Kamm are associated with this view. Ethical particularists, who do not believe in moral principles in the first place, are naturally inclined towards this view, too. While in principle conceivable, this would entail that arguments from moral irrelevance do not work at all, as they require that an intuition at a higher level of generality can override the case-specific intuitions. The third possibility is therefore not an option for proponents of arguments from moral irrelevance. These three ways of understanding the relation between general and case-specific intuitions are also distinguished in Kagan, 1998, pp. 13–14; Kamm, 1993, pp. 5–7.

136 Nye, 2015.

137 Singer, 1972, p. 236. The principle Singer refers to is: "[I]f it is in our power to prevent something very bad from happening, without thereby sacrificing anything of comparable moral importance, we ought, morally, to do it." (1972, p. 231). This raises an interpretative question: Is the duty to give to charity entailed by our obligation to save the drowning child and the moral irrelevance of spatial distance? Or is it directly entailed by the above principle (which would render the other argument obsolete)? I won't address this interpretative question here (refer e.g. to Nye, 2015, p. 630). Singer is inspired by Sidgwick (1981), another utilitarian who favors intuitions at a high level of generality.

138 Unger, 1997. Another skeptic about case-specific intuitions is Shelly Kagan (1989, pp. 13–15; 2016).

But this way of construing the relationship between the two types of intuitions would defeat the purpose of arguments from moral irrelevance. Arguments from moral irrelevance would then target precisely the sort of intuitions that are claimed to be rather irrelevant. For arguments from moral irrelevance to be dialectically forceful, it must be assumed that the targeted intuitions play a crucial role in the construction of moral theories. The fact that Greene attacks deontology by attacking case-specific deontological intuitions commits him to the view that these case-specific intuitions constitute the decisive evidence for deontology. It would be pointless to attack case-specific deontological intuitions if deontology rested primarily on more general intuitions. This has also been noted by Victor Kumar and Richmond Campbell, who point out that Greene's argument rests on the hidden "assumption [...] that the principal evidence for moral theories is our first order intuitions about concrete cases. One moral theory is more justified than another principally insofar as it better explains and systematizes our first order intuitions."[139] Presumably, what Greene has in mind is deontological theory that relies heavily on evidence from thought experiments involving the sort of dilemmas examined by Greene. The prototypical deontologist of this sort is Frances Kamm, who has practiced and encouraged the study of case-specific intuitions like no other. Her deontological views are based on a large set of carefully examined case-specific intuitions, and they are precisely the sort of case-specific intuitions that Greene seeks to undermine in an attempt to refute deontology.

But the assumption that case-specific intuitions constitute the principal evidence for deontology is in direct tension with the assumption that case-specific intuitions, as a rule, are much less reliable than more general ones. If the latter are more reliable than the former, it is them that provide the principal evidence for moral theories, rather than the unreliable case-specific ones. Assuming that general intuitions trump case-specific ones makes it easy to construct arguments from moral irrelevance and to maybe even challenge entire swathes of case-specific intuitions, such as all deontological intuitions. But it undermines the very force of these arguments, as they target intuitions that, ex hypothesi, should not play an important role in the construction of moral theories to begin with. It does not render these arguments invalid, but dialectically toothless. What Greene would have to do instead is attack deontological intuitions at a higher level of generality, such as, say, that the separateness of persons, the signing of con-

---

139 Kumar and Campbell, 2012, p. 313.

tracts, or the giving of promises are morally relevant factors.[140] It would be them that are crucial for the justification of deontology, not the case-specific intuitions that he is actually attacking.

To see the problem more clearly, consider how a deontologist might respond to Greene's challenge. A deontologist who accepts that case-specific intuitions are less reliable than general intuitions need not be too concerned about the finding that case-specific deontological intuitions are responsive to morally irrelevant factors. Her endorsement of deontology is motivated by intuitions at a higher level of generality anyway, precisely because she considers them more trustworthy than case-specific ones. By contrast, a deontologist who rests her case for deontology on case-specific intuitions, such as Kamm, will be loath to accept the assumption that we should always listen to our general intuitions rather than our case-specific ones when they are shown to clash.

That is, for arguments from moral irrelevance to have dialectical traction, it must be assumed that case-specific intuitions constitute an important source of evidence. But once we grant this, it becomes much more difficult (though not impossible) to debunk them by showing them to clash with an intuition at a higher level of generality. And there will always be the risk that our case-specific intuitions compel us to grant moral significance to factors that are irrelevant according to utilitarian principles.

So much for the first way in which arguments from moral irrelevance may backfire. Unfortunately for utilitarians, there are two more.

Second, then, arguments from moral irrelevance may backfire by undermining the utilitarian case-specific intuition. Greene's idea is that the utilitarian intuition and the general intuition are so compelling that they undermine the deontological intuition. But deontologists can retort that it is in fact the deontological intuition and the general intuition that are so compelling that, together, they undermine the utilitarian intuition. Again, which of the clashing intuitions should be dismissed depends arguably on their relative strengths, and deontologists can plausibly suggest that the utilitarian intuition is the weakest link (thus rejecting P4). For instance, they may argue that the intuition that one must not shove the heavy person off the bridge and the intuition that personal force is morally irrelevant entail that we should jettison the utilitarian intuition that it is morally permissible to hit the switch. In this way, the same evidence that Greene invokes in his attempt to debunk deontological intuitions could be invoked by deontologists to debunk utilitarian ones.

---

140 See also Berker, 2009, p. 325. Note that these intuitions possess independent intuitive plausibility, unlike perhaps the doctrine of double effect (Greene, 2014, p. 721).

It is easy to overlook this option, as one might take the empirical evidence to reveal that it is the deontological responses *rather than* the utilitarian responses that are responding to irrelevant factors.[141] But this is misleading. For whenever our case-specific responses vary in response to an irrelevant factor, *both* responses are sensitive to this irrelevant factor. The deontological intuition is triggered by the irrelevant factor that the victim is pushed rather than killed by hitting a switch. But the consequentialist intuition is likewise triggered by the irrelevant fact that the victim is killed by hitting a switch rather than pushed.[142] The empirical findings are symmetrical, so to speak. This is why the argument requires the additional premise P4, if it is to undermine the deontological intuition. And it is open to the deontologist to object that the deontological judgment is intuitively more compelling and should overrule the utilitarian one, rather than vice versa. Indeed, it is not too far-fetched to hold that the intuition that it is wrong to shove the heavy person off the bridge is more robust than the one that it is permissible to hit the switch.

A similar point has been made by Kumar and Campbell. They criticize Greene's argument on the grounds that the necessary additional assumption (P4) is too controversial, maintaining that it is not clear which way the conflict between the pair of conflicting case-specific intuitions should be resolved. They suggest drawing the more cautious conclusion "that we should withhold from drawing a moral distinction between the cases."[143] That is, we must stop at C2 and refrain from specifying which case-specific intuition should be dismissed. But things are worse for the utilitarian would-be debunker. The deontologist can insist that we *can* go beyond C2 because the deontological intuition may be so strong that it becomes clear that we should reject the utilitarian one.

Again, I am not so much concerned with showing that Greene's particular debunking arguments backfire than with suggesting that his method cannot easily be used to debunk deontological intuitions on a larger scale. Even if he should succeed at undermining the particular deontological intuition about the impermissibility of shoving the heavy person off the bridge, deontologists need not be too worried that the same method can be used to systematically undermine all or even the bulk of deontological case-specific intuitions.

The third way in which the argument backfires is a variation of the one just discussed. Deontologists can adopt the argument from moral irrelevance for

---

141 See e.g. Berker's characterization of the argument from moral irrelevance (2009, p. 321).
142 As correctly observed by Kumar and Campbell (2012, p. 317) and, at one point, by Greene (2014, p. 713).
143 Kumar and Campbell, 2012, p. 322. Note, though, that they have doubts about the accuracy of Greene's empirical findings.

their own purposes and turn it into a powerful anti-utilitarian argument. Selim Berker observes: "it is open to the defender of deontology to reply that, intuitively, the faculty eliciting consequentialist reactions is also responding to morally irrelevant factors, or failing to respond to morally relevant ones."[144] As Berker characterizes it, this parallel anti-consequentialist debunking argument takes the negative form, stating that utilitarian judgments *fail* to be sensitive to factors that *are* relevant. Here is just one example of how such a parallel argument might go: Consider *Child*, which is a variation of the traditional *Switch* dilemma except that the person on the sidetrack is your own child. Saving the five workers would require killing your own child. A critic of utilitarianism could plausibly argue that there *is* a morally relevant difference between *Switch* and *Child*, namely that the victim in *Child* is your own child. This is why the consequentialist response to *Child* fails to be sensitive to a morally relevant factor. Examples like this can easily be multiplied, as there are many factors apart from those bearing on the maximization of welfare that are widely felt to be normatively relevant. Berker, for instance, mentions the separateness of persons, a factor that is widely thought to possess great moral significance but that utilitarian theories notoriously fail to do justice to.[145]

This objection does not imply that Greene's attack on specific deontological intuitions fails. It may still be true that we should dismiss our intuition about the impermissibility of shoving the heavy person off the bridge. But it means that the same method can be used to debunk utilitarian responses, too.

Kumar and Campbell have come to the rescue of Greene by drawing attention to an asymmetry between Greene's anti-deontological argument and parallel anti-consequentialist arguments.[146] They observe that the latter are less effective because they rely on normative premises that are controversial, whereas Greene's argument invokes an intuition that even deontologists accept. No deontologist finds it intuitive that personal force makes a moral difference.[147] By contrast, utilitarians are (relatively) happy to assert that kinship – or indeed *any* factor that does not affect the maximization of welfare – is morally irrelevant. The anti-consequentialist argument thus threatens to beg the question against the consequentialist. Greene's argument, by contrast, is convincing even to deontologists. Kumar and Campbell have, I think, correctly identified an important strength of Greene's argument. It also means that Berker's claim that Greene's

---

144 Berker, 2009, p. 325.
145 Berker, 2009, p. 325.
146 Kumar and Campbell, 2012, pp. 314–315.
147 Greene, 2010, p. 14; 2014, pp. 711–713.

argument fails to "advance the dialectic on the relative merits of deontology versus consequentialism" is unfair.[148] It does advance the debate precisely because it rests on an assumption that even deontologists cannot dispute. At the same time, however, this asymmetry does not entirely defuse Berker's challenge. It does not mean that these parallel anti-consequentialist arguments are altogether without force so that utilitarians need not be concerned about them. Surely, the fact that a great many people intuit that utilitarian judgments fail to respond to morally relevant factors is a serious problem for utilitarians. An objection along these lines might not be particularly original and thus do less to 'advance the dialectic', but it cannot easily be dismissed, either.

Greene has acknowledged the problem that case-specific utilitarian judgments may fall victim to the same sort of debunking attack, and he has attempted to defuse this problem by appeal to dual-process theory. He maintains that dual-process theory predicts that only deontological intuitions are susceptible to the argument from morally (ir-)relevant factors. But his argument for this prediction is not convincing. Greene writes: "Why not suppose, as Berker does [...], that consequentialist 'intuitions' are as much to blame as deontological ones? The answer is that there is a deep cognitive asymmetry between consequentialist and deontological thinking, as posited by the dual-process theory."[149] He then goes on to explain that consequentialist responses are reasoned in that they involve the conscious application of a moral principle (that of maximizing welfare). By contrast, deontological intuitions are automatic and emotional, and when people give deontological responses, they are often unaware of the principles that govern their responses (e. g. the doctrine of double effect).[150] Indeed, consequentialist intuitions have been shown to be psychologically so unlike ordinary intuitions that they do not even qualify as intuitions in the psychological sense of the term. They are only intuitions in the philosopher's sense. And because they are so different, they are less likely to be vulnerable to the argument from moral irrelevance, as it casts doubt specifically on 'psychological' intuitions:

> In short, characteristically consequentialist judgments are not intuitive in the psychological sense, but characteristically deontological judgments are. [...] More generally, our mysteriously variable moral intuitions are a nuisance for consequentialists, but they are [...] the lifeblood of deontological theorizing. For these reasons, evidence that our intuitions [in

---

148 Berker, 2009, p. 326.
149 Greene, 2010, p. 18.
150 See in particular Cushman et al., 2006; Hauser et al., 2007. Note though that the evidence provided by these studies is rather mixed and limited.

the psychological sense] are unreliable is a point in favor of consequentialism and a point against deontology.[151]

The main steps of Greene's reasoning thus appear to be roughly as follows:

P1) The deontological responses that have been shown to be sensitive to morally irrelevant factors are based on 'psychological' intuitions.

P2) Utilitarian responses are not based on 'psychological' but 'philosophical' intuitions.

C) A parallel argument against utilitarian judgments is therefore unlikely to succeed.

But an argument along these lines, even when we fill in the gaps, is not convincing. To begin with, the argument presumes that the unreliability of deontological responses is due to their being driven by 'psychological' intuitions. And it is unclear whether this is the case. The fact that the unreliable intuitions are 'psychological' intuitions does not mean that they are unreliable *because* they are 'psychological' intuitions. Their 'psychological' nature could be completely unrelated to their sensitivity to irrelevant factors. The fact that utilitarian judgments differ psychologically from deontological judgments would then be beside the point. Greene does relatively little to explain why the fact that deontological intuitions are sensitive to morally irrelevant factors should be due to their being 'psychological' intuitions. If anything, he appears to suggest that the same considerations that underlie the functionalist argument explain why specifically 'psychological' intuitions are unreliable. However, as will become clear in the discussion of the functionalist argument, this is confused. The functionalist argument and the argument from moral irrelevance are on two different levels, and considerations underlying the former cannot inform latter.

But even if we could say that the sensitivity to irrelevant factors of deontological intuitions is due to their being 'psychological' intuitions, this would not allow us to rule out that utilitarian judgments may be vulnerable to a parallel argument. The fact that responses that are based on 'psychological' intuitions tend to be sensitive to irrelevant factors because they are based on 'psychological' intuitions simply does not entail that responses that are not based on 'psychological' intuitions are unlikely to be sensitive to irrelevant factors (or insensitive to relevant factors). For they may of course have this defect *in spite of* not being based on 'psychological' intuitions. And importantly, this is more than just a hypothetical possibility. As noted above, there are at least concrete reasons to suppose that some utilitarian judgments *are* insensitive to morally relevant fac-

---

151 Greene, 2010, p. 20.

tors. I am not here positively asserting that such factors as kinship *definitely are* morally relevant. Kumar and Campbell have rightly pointed out that such claims are to some extent controversial. Rather, my point is that these claims are at least *reasonably plausible*. They are too plausible to be brushed aside on the grounds that utilitarian responses differ psychologically from those intuitions that have already been experimentally demonstrated to be responsive to irrelevant factors. When a deontologist rejects some consequentialist judgment as failing to account for a morally relevant factor (e.g. kinship), it simply does not do to respond that this cannot be true because the judgment is not based on a psychological intuition. Appeals to what dual-process theory might predict about whether utilitarian judgments are open to a similar objection are simply way too speculative to be of any dialectical use in this situation.

The above analysis also confirms a worry first voiced by Berker that dual-process theory and the underlying neuroscientific findings play no role in the argument from moral irrelevance.[152] The argument relies exclusively on experimental findings regarding which factors trigger our intuitions. The neuroscientific findings and dual-process theory are completely peripheral to it. The attempt to use dual-process theory to defuse the backfiring problem fails.

3.4 The scope problem

The scope of the argument from moral irrelevance is further reduced by the paucity of the necessary empirical evidence. According to the argument from moral irrelevance, deontological intuitions must be distrusted because they can be shown to be sensitive to morally irrelevant factors. This argument requires empirical evidence to the effect that our deontological responses in fact are sensitive to factors that can readily be seen to be morally irrelevant. But so far, the evidence is rather meagre and mixed.

Greene's argument focuses on sacrificial dilemmas, but, again, intuitions about sacrificial dilemmas make up only a small portion of all deontological intuitions. We also have deontological intuitions about a large range of ethical issues that are unrelated to the kind of sacrificial questions examined by Greene. Clearly, the fact that some of our intuitions in sacrificial dilemmas seem to be responsive to irrelevant factors hardly allows drawing any general conclusions about the reliability of deontological intuitions. Greene states that he "favor[s]" the "possibility [...] that once all of the inner workings of our judgments are re-

---

152 Berker, 2009, pp. 325–326

vealed by science, there will be nothing left for deontologists. All of the factors that push us away from consequentialism will, once brought into the light, turn out to be things that we will all regard as morally irrelevant."[153] But this is distinctly unsatisfactory. While it is understandable that he 'favors' this possibility, this is as of now mere speculation with little concrete evidence to back it up. Indeed, as we have just seen, there is reason to assume that the opposite is true, and that the same method can be used to challenge consequentialist judgments.

Also, the evidence is again incomplete even with regard to deontological intuitions in sacrificial dilemmas.[154] The two factors singled out by Greene and his colleagues are not necessary criteria for the triggering of deontological intuitions in sacrificial dilemmas. Recall *Rifle*, *Hypnosis* and *Electroshock*. In none of these dilemmas, the force that directly impacts the victim is generated by the agent's muscles. The electric current in *Electroshock* is obviously not generated by the agent. In *Rifle*, the force that impacts the victim is generated by explosives. And *Hypnosis* does not involve any force at all. And yet these scenarios seem to elicit deontological intuitions.[155] We do not know which factors these intuitions are triggered by, but in theory it may turn out that these factors *are* morally relevant. Therefore, focusing on the moral (ir-)relevance of personal force and spatial distance will not get us far. In order to mount a complete argument from moral irrelevance that debunks all, or even the greater part, of deontological responses in sacrificial dilemmas, one must first identify *all* factors that deontological responses are sensitive to in such dilemmas, which so far has not been done, and which, one might add, would be a formidable task.[156]

Finally, and maybe most seriously, it is unclear to what extent intuitions that respond to the conjunction of personal force and intention really are sensitive to morally irrelevant factors. Greene focuses on the moral irrelevance of personal force, observing jokingly that, if we were consulted for moral advice on a sacri-

---

153 Greene, 2010, p. 21. He promises to offer more evidence in his book (2013), but as far as I can see the book includes no such evidence.

154 Greene has conceded that the personal-force-cum-intention theory is "incomplete" or "only an approximation" of the solution to the trolley problem (2016, p. 176).

155 In an endnote, Greene acknowledges the possibility that our 'alarm gizmo' might "learn to respond to other kinds of violence, such as gun violence" (2013, p. 378). But note that we do not know which factor in *Rifle* triggers the response. Is it the fact that it involves explosives, or the fact that it involves a gun, or the fact that it involves a hard metal object, or the fact that the victim is killed like game, or the fact that it involves a loud noise, or is it some other factor or even a combination of multiple factors?

156 Moreover, Railton has offered a counterexample suggesting that the two factors are also not sufficient to trigger a deontological response (2014, pp. 854–855). See also again Berker on possible counterexamples to Greene and colleagues' theory (2009, p. 323 n73).

ficial dilemma situation, we would not ask whether the dilemma involves pushing a person or hitting a switch. While this bit of the argument is convincing, it is
less clear whether the other factor, intention, is morally irrelevant, too. The doctrine of double effect, according to which there is a moral difference between
intending harm as a means to an end and merely foreseeing harm is a time-hon-
ored and widely endorsed philosophical view.[157] It can hardly be dismissed as
evidently mistaken in the same way as our sensitivity to personal force. This
means that the argument from moral irrelevance is seriously flawed. It may be
that one of two factors that jointly trigger deontological intuitions is morally irrelevant. But if the other *is* morally relevant, it means that a deontological intuition indicates that there *is* a morally relevant difference. A deontological intuition would be a sufficient but not necessary indicator of a morally relevant
difference. It is therefore difficult to see why deontological intuitions should
be dismissed as unreliable in light of their sensitivity to these two factors.

Greene's main responses to this problem is that there is an evolutionary
debunking explanation of why we feel that there is a moral difference between
intending harm and merely foreseeing harm as a side-effect.[158] According to
Greene, we are equipped with a cognitive subsystem that monitors our action
plans and that triggers an emotional alarm if these plans involve harm to another
individual. However, it would be too cognitively costly to inspect *all* causal effects of our actions. It therefore only inspects the main causal chain, namely
those events that are necessary for the achievement of the intended action.
This explanation constitutes an evolutionary debunking argument of why we
take the intended/foreseen distinction to be morally relevant: "Harms caused
as a means push our moral-emotional buttons not because they are objectively
worse but because the alarm system that keeps us from being casually violent
lacks the cognitive capacity to keep track of side effects."[159] Greene seeks to *combine* the argument from moral irrelevance with a new evolutionary debunking argument.[160]

This combination of the argument from moral irrelevance with an evolutionary debunking argument is problematic, as it means that the former cannot
serve as an alternative to the argument from evolutionary history. Greene

---

157 See McIntyre, 2014; for two contemporary defenses of this doctrine, refer to Quinn, 1993;
Wedgewood, 2011, see Lott, 2016.
158 Greene, 2010, p. 17; 2013, pp. 224–240; 2016, p. 176. Greene appears to offer a different response in Greene, 2014, p. 721, which has been convincingly dealt with by Lott (2016).
159 Greene, 2009, pp. 239–240.
160 It is new in that it played no role in the initial statement of the argument from evolutionary
history as discussed in the previous chapter.

seems to have developed the argument from moral irrelevance as a response to problems with the argument from evolutionary history. But if the argument from moral irrelevance is partially dependent on an evolutionary debunking explanation, too, nothing is gained by substituting the argument from moral irrelevance for the argument from evolutionary history. It would mean buying into the evolutionary debunking program after all, which, as we have seen, threatens to undermine utilitarianism, too.

3.5 How useful are experiments?

Arguments from moral irrelevance exist both in experimental and non-experimental versions. Greene's argument relies on experimental findings about which factors trigger people's intuitions. But it is also possible to identify the factors that our intuitions are sensitive to from the armchair and to use these findings to construct arguments from moral irrelevance.[161] As noted earlier, similar non-experimental versions of such arguments have been put forth by Singer and Unger. Greene, however, has presented his argument as an example of how experimental moral psychology can advance moral theorizing. It is supposed to demonstrate "that interesting scientific facts about moral psychology can, when combined with relatively uninteresting normative assumptions, lead us to relatively interesting normative conclusions."[162] Thus, in addition to debunking deontology, his goal is to demonstrate the normative significance of experimental moral psychology. I will conclude this chapter by explaining why this attempt at demonstrating the normative significance of experimental moral psychology is somewhat underwhelming. The use of experimental methods to construct arguments from moral irrelevance is at worst counterproductive and at best helpful but not game-changing.

My criticism will focus on experimental studies revealing people's sensitivity to what I call morally irrelevant *internal* factors. The involvement of personal force in a trolley scenario, for instance, is an internal feature of the scenario itself.[163] By contrast, some morally irrelevant factors that our intuitions are sensitive to are *external* to the moral scenarios. There are, for instance, studies suggesting that moral intuitions are responsive to the order of presentation, to hypnotic suggestion and to whether one is seated in a clean or dirty environ-

---

161 See again Campbell and Kumar, 2012 for a related discussion.
162 Greene, 2014, p. 771.
163 Other studies that have revealed sensitivity to morally irrelevant internal factors include Gino et al., 2010; Uhlmann et al., 2009.

ment.[164] These findings, too, identify morally irrelevant factors that our intuitions are sensitive to, but these factors are not features of the scenarios themselves. Rather, they pertain to the *presentation* of the dilemmas and are in this sense external. In what follows, I will only be concerned with studies revealing sensitivity to morally irrelevant internal factors.

The experimental studies invoked by Greene investigated laypeople's moral intuitions. His argument from moral irrelevance thus targets in the first instance laypeople's intuitions. The problem is that targeting laypeople's intuitions reduces the force of arguments from moral irrelevance. Deontologists can retort that it has not been shown that *their* deontological intuitions are sensitive to irrelevant factors, the intuitions of trained philosophers. And it is these expert intuitions that deontological theories are based upon. That is, deontologists can claim that philosophers' and laypeople's intuitions diverge and that the former can be expected to be less susceptible to morally irrelevant factors. In this case, an argument from moral irrelevance that relies on data about laypeople's intuitions will not put much pressure on advocates of the targeted theory

The notion that philosophers are expert intuiters is, of course, controversial.[165] The proponent of an argument from moral irrelevance that relies on data about laypeople's intuitions could reject the expertise claim, insisting that laypeople's and philosophers' intuitions are sensitive to exactly the same irrelevant factors. Whether this is the case is difficult to say. There are studies suggesting that philosophers' moral intuitions are equally sensitive to morally irrelevant *external* factors.[166] But as of yet there is no evidence concerning their sensitivity to morally irrelevant *internal* factors. To simply take for granted that the folk moral intuitions revealed by surveys are representative of those held by trained philosophers is risky. The expertise claim may itself be fairly speculative, but it possesses some prima facie plausibility. It therefore seems unwise, from a dialectical point of view, to attack a moral view, such as deontology, by attacking the layperson's version of it.

There is a related and somewhat more technical reason why specifically Greene's anti-deontological argument from moral irrelevance should have targeted philosophers' rather than laypeople's intuitions. One element of his argument

---

164 Liao et al., 2012; Petrinovich and O'Neill, 1996; Schnall et al., 2008; Schwitzgebel and Cushman, 2012, 2015; Tobia et al., 2013; Wheatley and Haidt, 2005; Wiegmann et al., 2012. In light of the replication crisis, findings like these should be taken with a grain of salt (see e. g. Landy and Goodwin, 2015).

165 See especially Weinberg et al., 2010, but also Kauppinen, 2014, p. 295.

166 Schwitzgebel and Cushman, 2012, 2015; Tobia et al. 2013a; Tobia et al., 2013b; Wiegmann et al., 2020.

against deontology is the allegation that more elaborate deontological theories are the output of confabulatory post hoc rationalization rather than that of unbiased and careful moral reflection. This argument from confabulation will be considered in more detail in Chapter 5. To anticipate somewhat, the allegation that deontologists are post hoc rationalizers is supported by two observations: First, there is ample empirical evidence that people routinely engage in confabulatory post hoc rationalization, such as Haidt's dumbfounding experiment.[167] Second, more elaborate deontological theories tend to confirm our deontological gut reactions: "For example, [...] there is a complicated, highly abstract theory of rights that explains why it's okay to sacrifice one life for five in the *trolley* case [i.e. the *Switch* case] but not in the *footbridge* case, and it *just so happens* that we have a strong negative emotional response to the latter case but not to the former."[168] Greene reckons that the best explanation of this striking coincidence is that deontologists are really just rationalizing their gut reactions. It is important to note that post hoc reasoning is epistemically problematic only when the relevant intuitions have been shown to be unreliable. If deontological intuitions about different trolley cases have been shown to be unreliable, the deontologist who is engaged in post hoc reasoning is trying to vindicate intuitions that there is no reason to assume to be correct. By contrast, should the deontological intuitions be reliable, the theories produced by deontologists might well provide accurate systematizations and explications of the intuited truths. But this means that Greene's argument from moral irrelevance, which is supposed to debunk deontological intuitions, must target those intuitions that the more elaborate deontological theories are allegedly rationalizations of. This is necessary for the argument from post hoc rationalization to work. And since the philosophers who have developed these elaborate deontological theories must surely be assumed to have rationalized their *own* intuitions, Greene's argument from moral irrelevance must target the intuitions of these philosophers. Therefore, if Greene's argument from moral irrelevance undermines laypeople's deontological intuitions rather than those of deontological philosophers, the attack on more elaborate deontological theories – a pivotal component of his attack on deontology – collapses. This collapse can be prevented by making the assumption that laypeople's and philosophers' intuitions are identical and thus sensitive to the same morally irrelevant factors. But this assumption is controversial, and Greene's argument had better not rest upon it.

---

167 See also Dutton and Aron, 1974; Gazzaniga and LeDoux, 1978; Nisbett and Wilson, 1977; Uhlmann et al., 2009; Wheatley and Haidt, 2005; T. D. Wilson, 2002; Wilson and Nisbett, 1978. **168** Greene, 2008, p. 68.

All this suggests that building arguments from moral irrelevance on experimental data about laypeople's intuitions is, in fact, counterproductive. Proponents of arguments from moral irrelevance, especially Greene, would be well-advised to target philosophers' intuitions rather than those of laypeople. This leaves them with two options. They can either use data gathered experimentally by surveying philosophers' intuitions or use data gathered in a collaborative armchair-based enterprise by philosophers. Both options capture philosophers' intuitions, but only the first option is truly experimental, whereas the second is conventional.

The first approach, that of testing philosophers' intuitions experimentally, strikes me as an interesting and worthwhile research project. But given the availability of the second option, such experiments are at least not indispensable for the construction of arguments from moral irrelevance. As mentioned above, this conventional method has in fact already been used to construct arguments from moral irrelevance, in particular by Unger. And, it may be added, in the works of such thinkers as Unger and Kamm, the conventional method of investigating our intuitions from the armchair has reached an admirable level of sophistication and precision.

The experimental approach may be credited with improving on the armchair-based one by correcting for biases and individual idiosyncrasies, thereby guaranteeing greater validity and generalizability. This may be true even taking into account that the armchair-based investigation of moral intuitions is often a collaborative effort by the philosophical community rather than an individual one. But experimental arguments from moral irrelevance still represent only a marginal improvement over traditional, non-experimental arguments from moral irrelevance. They do not constitute anything resembling a methodological breakthrough, contrary to what Greene insinuates.

The fact that experimental methods are not indispensable for the construction of arguments from moral irrelevance is worth highlighting, as it implies that Greene's empirical research is more or less redundant for the argument from moral irrelevance. Not only is the argument from moral irrelevance not supported by dual-process theory, as discussed above. It also does not strictly require experimental methods. Thus, besides facing the backfiring problem and the scope problem, the argument fails to show how empirical methods can advance moral theorizing.

Again, experimental studies revealing sensitivity to morally irrelevant external factors are exempt from this criticism. I find it difficult to see how philosophers could reliably find out about the influence of irrelevant external factors upon moral judgment from the armchair, precisely because these factors are external to the thought experiments proper. We need systematic and rigorous scientific experiments to discover that, say, hypnotic disgust or framing effects influence our moral intuitions. It seems, then, that experimental methods are much more indispensable to finding out about our sensitivity to morally irrelevant external factors and to arguments based on such findings.

4 Deontology, Utilitarianism, and Morality as Problem-Solving

4.1 Introduction

The third version of the primary argument makes the case for utilitarianism on the grounds of utilitarianism is better suited to solve our moral problems. Greene refers to it as the "indirect route"[169]; I call it the functionalist argument. The functionalist argument states that we should favor utilitarian over deontological solutions to unfamiliar moral problems because our automatic, deontological intuitions have not evolved to deal with such problems.

The functionalist argument avoids some of the pitfalls identified in the previous chapters. It is much less ambitious than the argument from evolutionary history and the argument from moral irrelevance. It is an argument for utilitarianism and against deontology, but only with regard to some moral problems. Indeed, it involves a partial vindication of deontology, namely as a solution to familiar moral problems. This contrasts with Greene's evolutionary skepticism about the reliability of our deontological intuitions and with his hope that the argument from moral irrelevance will eventually undermine all deontological intuitions. The limited scope of the functionalist argument is a feature, not a bug, in that it is not intended to undermine more than a specific subset of deontological intuitions. Moreover, unlike the argument from moral irrelevance, it rests squarely on dual-process theory and would, if successful, prove the normative significance of dual-process theory and the neuroscientific findings it is based on.

This chapter argues that it is not successful. It also explores the pitfalls of construing morality – both deontology and utilitarianism – in functionalist terms as a problem-solving device.[170]

4.2 The functionalist argument

The basic idea underlying the functionalist argument is that we are facing two types of moral problems – unfamiliar and familiar ones – that must be dealt

---

169 Greene, 2014; see also 2010, 2013, 2017. For some interesting discussions, see Dale, 2020; FitzPatrick, 2018; Kraaijeveld and Sauer, 2019; Lott, 2016; May, 2018, pp. 101–103; Paulo, 2019.
170 A similar 'functionalist' project is pursued by Kitcher (2011).

https://doi.org/10.1515/9783110750195-005

with in two different ways that correspond to the two processes identified by dual-process theory. Unfamiliar problems are those with which we have "inadequate evolutionary, cultural, or personal experience."[171] Familiar problems are those with which we have adequate such experience. When facing familiar moral problems, we can rely on our automatic, deontological gut reactions, because they have over time adjusted to these problems through evolutionary, cultural and personal learning processes. By contrast, when we are confronting peculiarly modern, unfamiliar problems, we must distrust our automatic mode and switch into the 'manual' mode, which yields utilitarian solutions.

The moral problems we are facing range from the difficulty of cooperative behavior in everyday life to more complex and/or recent problems such as violent conflict, global warming, terrorists using weapons of mass destruction, global poverty, bioethical problems, the place of religion in public live, capital punishment, abortion, and so forth.[172] Familiar problems are often what Greene calls 'Me vs Us' problems. These are problems associated with conflicts between individuals within the same group. In order to reap the benefits of cooperation, individuals must sometimes restrain their own selfishness, especially in prisoner's dilemma-like situations. Morality enables cooperation in these situations by telling people to put 'Us' ahead of 'Me'. Unfamiliar problems, by contrast, are often of the 'Us vs Them' type. They concern conflicts between groups. 'Us vs Them' problems have two dimensions: "First, there is plain old selfishness at the group level, also known as *tribalism*. Humans nearly always put Us ahead of Them. Second, beyond tribalism, groups have genuine differences in values, disagreements concerning the proper *terms* of cooperation."[173] And both sub-problems entail costly inter-tribal conflicts.[174] Problems arising from recent technological or social developments – e. g. bioethical problems – are also typical examples of unfamiliar problems.

Here is a rough summary of the functionalist argument:

The Functionalist Argument

P1) We are facing two types of moral problems, familiar and unfamiliar ones.

P2) Our moral cognition operates in two modes, an automatic and a manual mode.

---

171 Greene, 2014, p. 714.
172 See e. g. Greene, 2013, pp. 98–99, 348; 2017, p. 73.
173 Greene, 2013, pp. 66–67, see also p. 99; 2017, pp. 72–73. His characterization of 'Us vs Them' problems as 'unfamiliar' is problematic, though (see note 185 below).
174 Greene, 2013, pp. 1–27, 293–295.

P3) Our automatic mode has evolved to deal with familiar problems but not with unfamiliar ones.

P4) The automatic mode yields deontological judgments, and the manual mode yields consequentialist ones.

P5) We can rely on our automatic responses only when facing problems that these responses have evolved to deal with.

C) We can rely on our automatic, deontological responses when dealing with familiar problems but must switch to manual, consequentialist reasoning when dealing with unfamiliar problems.

4.3 Begging the question

To begin with, it is important to note that Greene has, somewhat surreptitiously, shifted the topic of his inquiry. The functionalist argument is meant to determine which moral norms we should adopt in order to achieve certain pre-defined goals. The suggestion to rely on our automatic, deontological responses in familiar but not in unfamiliar situations is best understood as a heuristic.[175] By contrast, both the argument from evolutionary history and the argument from moral irrelevance are attempts to identify the moral goals we should try to achieve in the first place. This also explains why the conclusions of these arguments differ. The functionalist argument is much more conciliatory than the other two arguments in that it explicitly acknowledges the reliability of some deontological intuitions.

Since the functionalist argument is about achieving moral goals, it already presupposes answers to contested moral questions. When we ask what norms best serve a given purpose, we are asking an essentially *instrumental* question.[176] This implies that we must already have an idea of what our final (non-instrumental) goals ought to be. The functionalist argument does therefore not provide an answer to the deontology/utilitarianism controversy, understood as a controversy about what is finally morally valuable. Rather, it *presupposes* an answer to this question. This issue is less serious when the moral problems identified by Greene are generally agreed to really be problems. For instance, deontologists and util-

---

175 Bruni et al. call this the 'collective usefulness' view: "According to this view, certain forms of moral thinking are to be recommended because they serve instrumentally to further widely shared goals, such as a reduction in conflict, or an increase in social cohesion." (2014, p. 106). Note that there is a long tradition in utilitarian thought of embracing at least some common-sense moral rules as useful rules-of-thumb (Sunstein, 2005, p. 533).
176 See note 175 above.

itarians alike can agree that weapons of mass destruction and climate change *are* problems, so there is nothing question begging about maintaining that we must find ways of overcoming *these* problems. But as soon as we turn to more controversial issues – especially those contested between deontologists and utilitarians – the functionalist approach threatens to beg the question.[177]

4.4 Internal inconsistencies

Another problem is that Greene does not seem to be sufficiently aware of the discontinuity between the functionalist argument and the other versions of the primary argument. This is evidenced by how Greene characterizes the relation between the argument from moral irrelevance and the functionalist argument. The argument from moral irrelevance is clearly informed by a conventional rather than a functionalist approach to morality. The factor 'personal force' is dismissed as lacking *intrinsic* moral significance rather than as being irrelevant with regard to the achievement of cooperation (or some other moral goal). This means that the genealogical considerations that underlie the functionalist argument do not predict that (or explain why) deontological responses are sensitive to factors that strike us as morally irrelevant. This, however, is what Greene appears to be insinuating. He seems to think of the 'indirect' route as an expansion or elaboration of the 'direct route' (the argument from moral irrelevance). The latter allowed "[l]imited progress", whereas the former offers "a more general theory that tells us when our judgments are likely to go astray."[178] But this is confused. The genealogical considerations that inform the functionalist argument predict, for instance, that our intuitive responses foster within-group cooperation while hindering between-group cooperation. Our conception of moral relevance, however, is distinct from the question of what is instrumentally necessary for the achievement of cooperation. Therefore, the genealogical considerations underlying the functionalist argument imply nothing about our intuitions' sensitivity to morally irrelevant factors.

It might be possible to disentangle these two arguments and to assign each a meaningful role in the overall structure of the argument. But Greene's own understanding and presentation of how the functionalist argument relates to the

---

177 Greene seems to be aware of this problem and promises to address it in his book (2010, p. 24). But as I explain below, I find his treatment of these issues in his book unconvincing.
178 Greene, 2014, p. 713. Elsewhere, he writes that "whether a judgment is produced by a process that is emotional, heuristic, or a by-product of our evolutionary history is not unrelated to whether that judgment reflects a sensitivity to factors that are morally irrelevant." (2010, p. 12)

rest of his empirically informed case for utilitarianism seems confused. This confusion is also apparent in his discussion of Haidt's incest thought experiment, one of Greene's favored illustrations of how science can advance moral philosophy. Greene's argument is based on the plausible causal premise that people tend to condemn incest – such as the romantic affair between Julie and Mark – because incest led to genetic defects in the environment in which our ancestors evolved. He then maintains that "[w]hether or not a behavior increased the probability of deleterious consequences in the environment of our ancestors is irrelevant to its present moral acceptability, so long as this behavior does not also causes [*sic*] similar harm in our present environment" (which includes methods of birth control).[179] This leads him to conclude that we ought not condemn their behavior. While this may be true, Greene presents this as an illustration of the argument from moral irrelevance. He writes that the causal premise "tells us that people's judgments are, in this instance, determined by their sensitivity to a morally irrelevant factor."[180] But the causal premise does not specify the factors that trigger the deontological response. Our intuitive aversion to incestuous relationships is not sensitive to this evolutionary fact in the same manner in which our moral judgments are sensitive to personal force. Rather, what is triggering it is probably simply the fact that it is siblings rather than unrelated people who are having a love affair. The incest example is thus either an instance of the functionalist argument (as Greene appears to suggest elsewhere[181]) or of the argument from evolutionary history.

4.5 How functional are deontological intuitions?

Furthermore, his suggestion that our automatic, deontological responses are reliable in 'familiar' situations is very questionable. Greene reasons that "[a]utomatic settings can function well only when they have been shaped by *trial-and-error experience*", be it a biological, cultural or personal one.[182] But this reasoning rests on the problematic assumption that the criterion of selection of these

---

179 Greene, 2010, p. 11.
180 Greene, 2010, p. 11. Shortly after, he explicitly endorses the 'argument from moral irrelevance'-interpretation suggested by Berker. And he writes that his characterization of the argument from moral irrelevance is modelled on the incest argument (p. 15). Elsewhere (2014, p. 712), his presentation of the incest case is also embedded in a discussion of the argument from moral irrelevance.
181 Greene, 2010, p. 22.
182 Greene, 2014, p. 714.

mechanisms is whether a response helps us solve our moral problems.[183] This is roughly true of biological evolution, although only indirectly: Biological evolution does not select for moral dispositions that solve our moral problems but for dispositions that enhance our fitness. But since cooperative traits increase fitness and since lack of cooperation is one of the to-be-solved problems, our naturally evolved moral dispositions may be expected to provide decent solutions to some of our familiar moral problems. The case of cultural evolution, by contrast, is much trickier. It is fair to say that the laws of cultural transmission are still poorly understood. But according to one recent suggestion, informed by the so-called epidemiological approach, the 'cultural fitness' of a moral norm is a function of the following three factors:

(i) It yields material benefit to its believers or to the members of a culture who are in a position to indoctrinate others;

(ii) it is situated in a narrative context that is easy to learn because, e. g., it integrates with existing beliefs about the nature of the world or captures the imagination; or

(iii) it has emotional appeal, due to the intrinsic content of the belief or accompanying practices, such as emotional conditioning or emotionally intense religious rituals.[184]

Of these three factors, only the first factor might plausibly be connected to the resolution of moral problems. But even this is doubtful. For one thing, if some norms exist because they benefit the powerful indoctrinators, they are probably poorly aligned with the correct moral values. They do not solve our moral problems but the prudential problems of the powerful indoctrinators, so to speak. For another, if a norm benefits only the believers, this is bound to happen at the expense of members of the outgroup. It is, for instance, beneficial to believe that it is morally permissible to kill, enslave or, indeed, eat members of the outgroup.[185] Finally, to describe our personal learning experience as an adaptive 'trial-and-error process' strikes me as misleading, too. For when we make a bad moral judg-

---

183 This is also noted by Greene (2014, p. 714).

184 Prinz, 2007, p. 220. The epidemiological approach was pioneered by Dan Sperber (1996) and bears a resemblance to Dawkins and Dennett's meme theory mentioned in the introduction.

185 See Prinz, 2007, pp. 223–229. Greene could object that this is an *inter*-tribal conflict and as such not suited for our automatic mode, anyway. Indeed, at one point, Greene writes: "Of course, Us versus Them is a very old problem. But historically it's been a tactical problem rather than a moral one." (2013, p. 15) But this statement is puzzling. What does it mean for a problem to be a tactical rather than moral one? And why is the *intra*-tribal tragedy of the commons (presumably as 'tactical' a problem as one can imagine) a moral problem rather than a tactical one? And does this mean that 'familiarity' is *not* the decisive criterion, at least not the only one? In any case, even if we abstract from this specific problem with the cultural trial-and-error process, other problems remain.

ment (say, that the above incestuous relationship is a moral abomination), we do not get an 'error message' that prompts us to adjust our judgment. Greene likens the personal moral learning experience to learning to fear hot stoves by touching them.[186] But there is no obvious equivalent to the sensation of heat when we make a wrong moral judgment. You can go your entire life and never notice that you were wrong about abortion, incest, capital punishment, and so forth. In fact, a whole lot of people *do* go their entire lives without noticing that they have been wrong about these issues (whatever the truth about these issues may be).

All this is not to deny that there is some truth in Greene's idea that our automatic responses to familiar problems may contain acquired moral wisdom.[187] But the extent to which they do is unclear. The three learning mechanisms are much less linear and reliable than Greene's talk of a trial-and-error process suggests. The heuristic to use the automatic mode in familiar situations will probably misfire.[188]

4.6 How functional is utilitarianism?

Most worryingly, his positive case for utilitarianism seems confused. Even if we agree that our deontological responses fail us in unfamiliar situations because they have not evolved to deal with these situations, this still does not mean that manual mode reasoning yields good solutions to these problems. And this is because when we engage in manual moral reasoning, we typically do not engage in the kind of functionalist or instrumentalist reasoning that seeks to find 'solutions' to predefined 'problems'. When we contemplate a moral question ("Should I shove the heavy person off the bridge?", "Should we take money from the rich and give it to the poor?", etc.), we are not asking ourselves which steps must be taken to achieve some pre-defined moral goal, such as cooperation. Rather, moral deliberation centrally involves figuring out what is morally valuable in the first place, that is, what our moral goals should be and what moral side constraints we might have to respect. Manual moral reasoning is thus typically concerned with answering a different question than the one that is central to Greene's functionalist argument. Even if manual mode reasoning should support utilitarianism, this would not show that utilitarianism provides

---

186 Greene, 2014, p. 714.
187 See Railton, 2014 and Sauer, 2012a.
188 Similarly, Bruni et al. conclude that Greene's suggested heuristic is unconvincing until it has been corroborated by "a very ambitious empirical research program" (2014, p. 171).

workable 'solutions' to our moral 'problems'. If anything, it would show that the maximization of welfare is the only thing that matters morally. But this tells us little about how exactly to achieve, say, inter-tribal cooperation. In order to come up with solutions to unfamiliar problems, we would instead have to switch into the 'social scientist mode', so to speak, which engages in means-end reasoning and which might tell us how to best achieve inter-tribal cooperation and other goals.

The fact (if it is a fact) that 'manual' moral reasoning supports utilitarianism does therefore not constitute a functionalist vindication of utilitarianism. In his *Moral Tribes*, Greene offers two other rationales for choosing utilitarianism as the solution to unfamiliar moral problems.

One is that we should take a pragmatic approach and look out for what he calls a metamorality. This is a moral system that allows adjudicating inter-tribal conflicts because it is based on shared moral values: "This is the essence of deep pragmatism: to seek common ground not where we think it ought to be, but where it actually is."[189] And Greene believes that utilitarianism is particularly well suited to serve as such a metamorality.

The other is that utilitarianism is supported by rational, empirically informed moral theorizing. While he does not directly argue for the *truth* of utilitarianism, he contends that utilitarianism becomes "uniquely attractive once our moral thinking has been *objectively improved* by a scientific understanding of morality."[190] And by this he means that utilitarianism is supported by the argument from moral irrelevance[191] and evolutionary debunking arguments[192], alongside a range of other considerations.

It is easy to be confused by Greene's argumentation. One problem is that the above two criteria are in conflict with each other. If we 'objectively improve' our moral thinking in the way Greene envisages, we are bound to move away from the 'common ground where it actually is'. After all, 'objective improvement' involves, among other things, debunking generally shared deontological intuitions, which is the opposite of starting from common ground where it actually is. Relatedly, it is rather implausible to claim that utilitarianism, which has notoriously counterintuitive implications, rests on an overlapping moral consensus.[193] Thus, either we solve unfamiliar problems by appeal to commonly shared

---

189 Greene, 2013, p. 291.
190 Greene, 2013, p. 189.
191 Greene, 2013, pp. 213–217, 261.
192 Greene, 2013, pp. 224–245. Notice that the evolutionary debunking arguments that feature in Greene's book differ from Greene's earlier evolutionary debunking arguments.
193 Similarly, Wielenberg, 2014, p. 914.

values, in which case utilitarianism will hardly be our morality of choice. Or we solve these problems by relying on 'objectively improved moral thinking'. This method might vindicate utilitarianism, but it will not yield a metamorality based on shared values.

What is more, the rationale behind objectively improving our moral thinking is, in this context, itself rather puzzling. If we are interested in whether norms are conducive to solving pre-defined moral problems, the notion of objectively improving moral thinking as Greene conceives it is difficult to make sense of. Although Greene is reluctant to call this objectively improved morality (utilitarianism) *true*, his argument that empirically informed moral theorizing vindicates utilitarianism proceeds *as though* he was arguing for its truth. For instance, the argument from moral irrelevance purports to show that deontological intuitions are not tracking morally significant properties. Other of his arguments are supposed to dispel the impression that utilitarianism has counterintuitive implications.[194] But these considerations are meaningless or irrelevant from the functionalist vantage point. What matters from the functionalist vantage point is whether a given system of moral norms is *functional*, that is to say, whether it helps us overcome our moral problems. It may be true that objectively improved moral thinking supports utilitarianism. But given the functionalist framework, it is unintelligible why we should care about which morality is supported by objectively improved moral thinking in the first place.[195] This undermines Greene's empirically informed case for utilitarianism as the solution to our most pressing moral problems.

4.7 The uselessness of the suggested 'solution'

Finally, Greene's suggested solution – utilitarianism – is to some extent arbitrary and in fact not even that much of a solution. It is to some extent arbitrary because there are other norms or instructions that can serve the same function just as well as utilitarianism. Take 'Us vs. Them' problems, that is, inter-tribal conflicts arising from selfishness at the group level and differences in values. If this is the problem, we might as well simply establish moral norms that tell

---

194 Greene, 2013, pp. 254–285.
195 Similarly, Tobia, 2015, p. 749. By contrast, the idea behind seeking shared ground *is* intelligible. Given that one of the to-be-solved problems are the conflicts resulting from disagreement, identifying shared values may be a way of mitigating these conflicts. Interestingly, however, Greene himself appears to favor an epistemological rationale, which is less intelligible given the functionalist framework (2013, pp. 188–189).

people 1) to avoid in-group-favoritism and be generous towards the outgroup, and 2) to be respectful or tolerant of the views and practices of other 'tribes'. These two norms would be the most obvious and straightforward moral solutions to these problems. Similar *ad hoc* solutions can easily be formulated for other problems that Greene thinks need to be solved. There seems to be no need to accept a grand moral theory such as utilitarianism. And this points to the other problem: it is doubtful whether utilitarianism, or any *ad hoc* norm of the above sort, really qualifies as a 'solution'. For the problem is not so much that we do not know which norms, if complied with, would solve our 'moral problems'. As just seen, it should not be too difficult to formulate norms that fit this description. Rather, the main problem is the compliance itself, that is, getting people to actually do the things that need to be done in order to overcome the problems. It is instructive here to compare Greene's proposal to that of Ingmar Persson and Julian Savulescu, who start from a very similar diagnosis. They, too, are concerned that commonsense morality, evolved as a solution to the cooperation problems of relatively small groups, has become dysfunctional as a result of recent technological developments. Persson and Savulescu are particularly concerned about weapons of mass destruction and climate change. Their suggested solution, however, is the biological enhancement of people's moral *motivation*. And this makes more sense. Although compliance with some moral system such as, say, utilitarianism would certainly prevent the use of weapons of mass destruction, the exhortation to accept utilitarianism (and, by implication, to refrain from mass murder) would do very little to avert the use of such weapons. It will simply not be heeded. Likewise, the proposal to settle inter-tribal ideological conflicts by converging on utilitarianism as a shared morality is just too unlikely to gain sufficient traction among the members of the various ideological camps to actually qualify as a 'solution'. Few policy makers will be impressed with the suggestion to resolve conflicts between, say, Christians and Muslims by encouraging them to jointly embrace utilitarianism. At least with regard to some of the problems in question, Greene's solution is arguably a case of what David Estlund has called hopelessly aspirational theory. Hopelessly aspirational theory gives normative instructions that *could* be complied with but that we know *will not* be complied with. While hopelessly aspirational theory may be philosophically legitimate, as Estlund believes, it is just not the kind of solution we are looking for when we actually want to solve real-life problems.[196]

---

196 Estlund, 2014; Persson and Savulescu, 2012.

In summary, the functionalist argument raises more questions than it answers and is plagued by internal tensions and incongruities. At least in its current form, it does not constitute a compelling way of extracting normative conclusions from dual-process theory nor of establishing utilitarianism. Whether an improved version of the argument might allow deriving useful moral heuristics from dual-process theory remains to be seen.

5 Deontology, Confabulation, and the Structure of Philosophical Debate

5.1 Introduction

The argument from confabulation, which completes the debunking of deontology, is philosophically perhaps the most interesting moral debunking argument. In a nutshell, it asserts that deontological theory is the product of confabulatory post hoc rationalization. It is philosophically so interesting because it can teach us about the nature of debunking arguments, the structure of philosophical debate, and the place of genealogical reasoning in it. This chapter, by providing an analysis of the argument from confabulation, attempts to do just that. Besides offering a critical assessment of Greene and Singer's attempt to debunking deontology as confabulation, it seeks to achieve a better understanding of the place of genealogical reasoning in philosophical debate and to explain why some debunking arguments are permissible in philosophical debates and others are not.

5.2 The argument from confabulation

It is best to begin by reiterating why the primary argument does not yet amount to a complete refutation of deontology. The first part of the argument, if successful, debunks our emotion-driven deontological intuitions. However, as Greene and Singer acknowledge, deontological moral theory is more than just the unreflective articulation of these automatic deontological gut feelings. Deontologists have produced a host of extremely subtle and sophisticated philosophical defenses of deontology that do not rest on the debunked automatic and emotion-driven intuitions. These more 'cognitive' defenses of deontology survive the primary argument unscathed. Even if the primary argument succeeds, deontology has not been fully debunked. The crucial point, then, is that deontology is supported by more than just one line of argument. First, it is supported by our automatic, emotion-driven deontological intuitions, and second, it seems to be supported by more subtle and sophisticated philosophical arguments, which are, on the face of it, independent from our automatic, emotion-driven deontological intuitions. Even if the first line of argument is defeated, deontologists can still appeal to the second, independent support for deontology. This independent support for deontology may, of course, itself consist in normative intuitions as long as these intuitions are not among the ones that are the target of the primary

https://doi.org/10.1515/9783110750195-006

argument. That is, they must be intuitions that do not fall victim to the primary argument.[197]

To understand all this better, let us consider one concrete deontological doctrine in more detail. A good example may be retributivism, which is also discussed by Greene.[198] Retributivism is a backward-looking theory of punishment. Its regards punishment as a fitting response to some wrongdoing in the past irrespective of whether it has any positive consequences in the future. It thus contrasts with consequentialist theories of punishment, which are forward-looking in that they justify punishment by appeal to its beneficial effects in the future.[199] Some retributivists justify retributivism simply by appealing to the strong common-sense intuition that culpable wrongdoers deserve to suffer.[200] No attempt is being made to deduce the retributive principle from more general moral principles that explain why wrongdoers deserve to suffer. All the justificatory work is done by our brute retributivist intuitions. Others, by contrast, provide more elaborate justifications of retributivism by offering a rationale for exactly why retributive punishment is a fitting response to culpable wrongdoing. Here is one example of such an independent rationale for retributive punishment:

> Correct values are themselves without causal power, and the wrongdoer chooses not to give them effect in his life. So others must give them some effect in his life, in a secondary way. When he undergoes punishment these correct values are not totally without effect in his life (even though he does not follow them), because we hit him over the head with them. Through punishment, we give the correct values, qua correct values, some significant effect in his life, willy-nilly linking him up to them.[201]

This argument for retributive punishment, suggested by Robert Nozick, goes beyond merely insisting that wrongdoers intuitively deserve to suffer. It provides a deeper explanation of why they deserve to suffer, saying something about the effect that the correct values ought to have in people's lives and about how punishment can enforce this effect. Now, to refute retributivism, it does not suffice to present a debunking explanation of our brute intuition that wrongdoers deserve to suffer. While this may defeat the first set of evidence in support of retributi-

---

197 This is not to deny that these intuitions might be vulnerable to some other debunking argument. But that they are debunkable, too, would of course have to be demonstrated by Greene and Singer.

198 Greene, 2008, pp. 50–55, 59–66.

199 See Boonin, 2008, p. 85.

200 A case in point may be Kershnar, 2000.

201 Nozick, 1981, p. 375.

vism, retributivists could retort that they have independent evidence in support of retributivism, such as the argument presented by Nozick.

The function of the secondary argument, then, is to undermine evidence of such independent evidence in support of deontology. It is worth emphasizing how important this second part of the argument is. Given that much of deontological theory is fairly sophisticated rather than straightforwardly reliant on popular intuitions, the first part of the argument on its own achieves rather little. It defeats only a subset of the arguments that have been offered in defense of deontological views in moral theory. Deontologists who have advanced – or who have been swayed by – more subtle and refined arguments in favor of deontology need not be troubled by the primary argument and may reply 'So what?'. The question whether Greene and Singer succeed in undermining more sophisticated defenses of deontology is therefore of great dialectical importance. As a side note, this is also why naturalistic explanations of religious belief may fall short of debunking religious belief. As pointed out in the introduction of this book, genealogical debunking arguments are popular among critics of religion. Religious belief is dismissed as merely the result of evolutionary or cultural selection processes. However, while such naturalistic explanations might undermine brute religious feelings or intuitions as evidence of some supernatural being, they cannot on their own disprove the countless independent arguments for the existence of God. A believer could accept such naturalistic explanations of religious belief but appeal to these independent arguments for God's existence. To defeat the evidence of such independent reasons to believe in God, one would have to follow Greene and Singer's strategy and allege that these independent arguments are merely exercises in post hoc rationalization.[202]

Returning to deontology, the reason why the existence of more sophisticated arguments for deontology does not save deontology is that they must be assumed to be mere post hoc rationalizations of our deontological gut reactions, or so the secondary argument claims. Greene and Singer invoke Jonathan Haidt's social-intuitionist model, according to which moral judgments are based on quick gut reactions and followed by post hoc rationalization. However, while Haidt assumes that virtually all moral judgment follows this logic (deontological and consequentialist alike), Greene and Singer contend that it applies to deontology but not to consequentialism. After all, the dual-process account of moral judgment has it that only deontological judgments are prompted by automatic emotional reactions, whereas consequentialists judgments are formed in a more reasoned and dispassionate way. So unlike consequentialists, deontolo-

---

202 Thurow, 2013, pp. 91–97; see also Leben, 2014, pp. 341–346.

gists first make their judgments based on automatic gut reactions and then look out for reasons that may be appealed to to justify their intuitive deontological judgments

> Deontology, then, is a kind of moral confabulation. We have strong feelings that tell us in clear and [certain] terms that some things *simply cannot be done* and that other things simply must be done. But it is not obvious how to make sense of these feelings, and so we, with the help of some especially creative philosophers, make up a rationally appealing story.[203]

As anticipated above, this empirical hypothesis is supported by two different pieces of evidence.

First, it is supported by the fact that there is ample empirical evidence that people are generally prone to post hoc rationalization, both in moral and non-moral context.[204] It might be objected at this point that it is unclear whether the extant evidence tells us much about the tendency of trained philosophers to engage in confabulatory post hoc rationalization. It does not seem unreasonable to expect that expert thinkers are less prone to such irrational behavior than the subjects tested in these studies (some of which even suffered from brain damages). More recent studies, however, have found that trained philosophers tend to engage in moral post hoc rationalization just as much. Indeed, there is even some evidence suggesting that trained philosophers are *more* likely to engage in confabulatory post hoc rationalization than philosophical laypeople.[205] It is unlikely that deontologists can defuse this challenge by denying that philosophers are prone to rationalize moral intuitions.

The second piece of evidence is the fact that it would be an extraordinary coincidence if unbiased rational deliberation just so happened to turn out to confirm our deontological gut reactions. Given that post hoc rationalization is a common phenomenon and given the unlikelihood of this coincidence, post hoc rationalization is by far the best explanation of why moral philosophers have claimed there to be independent support for what our deontological gut reaction suggest, or so Greene and Singer's reasoning goes. To illustrate this point, Greene presents the story of Alice: According to Alice's own account, her evaluation of potential romantic partners is based on such attributes as their intel-

---

203 Greene, 2008, p. 63; see also pp. 36, 60–72; 2010, p. 24; 2013, pp. 298–301; 2014, pp. 718–725; Singer, 2005, pp. 349–350.
204 See again Dutton and Aron, 1974; Gazzaniga and LeDoux, 1978; Haidt et al., 2000; Nisbett and Wilson, 1977; Uhlmann et al., 2009; Wheatley and Haidt, 2005; T. D. Wilson, 2002; Wilson and Nisbett, 1978.
205 Schwitzgebel and Cushman, 2012, 2015; Schwitzgebel and Ellis, 2017.

ligence, their sense of humor, their likability, and so on. Strangely enough, though, her judgments happen to be perfectly predicted by the men's heights. Given the well-documented human tendency to engage in confabulatory post hoc rationalization, the most plausible interpretation of these 'data' is that her judgments are really determined by a preference for tall men while her own explanations of her judgments are merely post hoc rationalizations. Greene believes that deontological philosophers are like Alice. Just as Alice's preference is predicted by the men's heights, so the claims of deontological theorists are predicted by their moral gut reactions. This suggests that they are really just engaged in post hoc rationalization, just like Alice.

Greene and Singer thus, not entirely implausibly, argue that deontologists have probably misjudged the evidence in favor of deontology and that there is therefore little reason to assume that there really is independent support for deontology. The basic structure of the argument looks as follows:

The Argument from Confabulation

P1) Elaborate arguments for deontology are probably the result of confabulatory post hoc rationalization.

P2) If some arguments are probably the result of confabulatory post hoc rationalization, the evidence provided by these arguments is defeated.

C) Elaborate arguments for deontology do not provide evidence for the correctness of deontology.

As mentioned earlier, this reasoning works only if the initial emotion-based intuitions can be dismissed as unreliable, for instance, because they have been distorted by evolutionary forces or because they are responsive to morally irrelevant factors. In this case, post hoc reasoning is the attempt to find arguments for a view that there is no reason to assume to be correct. By implication, there is no reason to assume that these arguments are correct.[206] By contrast, if our au-

---

[206] The following passage captures well the interplay of these two elements in Greene and Singer's argument: "Of course it's possible that there is a coincidence here. It could be that it's part of the rationally discoverable moral truth that people really do deserve to be punished as an end in itself. At the same time, it could *just so happen* that natural selection, in devising an efficient means for promoting biologically advantageous consequences, furnished us with emotionally based dispositions that lead us to this conclusion; but this seems unlikely. Rather, it seems that retributivist theories of punishment are just rationalizations for our retributivist feelings, and that these feelings only exist because of the morally irrelevant constraints placed on natural selection in designing creatures that behave in fitness-enhancing ways. In other words, the natural history of our retributivist dispositions makes it unlikely that they reflect any sort of deep moral truth." (Greene, 2008, p. 71).

tomatic, emotion-based reactions are sound, say because they are the result of some kind of learning process, post hoc justification need not be confabulatory. Post hoc justification may then just be the ex post articulation of actual justificatory reasons, which our intuitions are reliably attuned to. For instance, if our intuition that wrongdoers deserve punishment were correct, post hoc reasoning could well lead us to discover (or recall) why this is actually the case.[207]

Greene and Singer, however, by first debunking the deontological intuitions that are being 'chased', seek to rule out such an optimistic interpretation of deontological post hoc rationalization. In this combination of primary and secondary argument resides the strength of the anti-deontological debunking project. The primary argument is not only supposed to undermine our deontological intuitions; it also makes it very likely that post hoc reasoning is confabulatory.

The combined debunking argument, consisting of the primary and the secondary debunking argument, thus (ideally) defeats both sets of evidence in support of deontology. It defeats the evidential status of our brute deontological intuitions, and it shows that there is little reason to assume that any of the more refined arguments in support of deontology are sound. As is characteristic of debunking arguments, this combined debunking argument falls short of establishing that deontology is false. If successful, it merely establishes that there is no positive reason to believe that deontology is correct.

It is crucial to notice that the primary and the secondary argument differ in the way in which they defeat the evidence in support of deontology. The primary argument provides an ordinary undercutting defeater. Undercutting defeaters remove the evidential force of some piece of evidence that had been taken to support some proposition.[208] The primary argument removes the evidential force of deontological intuitions, which had been thought to support deontology. The secondary argument, by contrast, relies on defeat based on what has come to be called higher-order evidence. Higher-order evidence is "evidence about the char-

---

207 As one commentator has correctly observed: "Only when we presuppose the unreliability of intuitions i.e. that they track morally irrelevant features, does rationalization go astray. Suppose that intuitions were reliable, as some believe. In this case, rationalization would not lack objective merit. Indeed, it would actually serve to organise a pattern of morally relevant features, as tracked by our intuitions. Rationalization understood as a process of finding intuitive patterns can, nevertheless, be poorly done, but it does not follow that the process per se is unreliable. Thus, calling deontology a rationalization in this sense is not a debunking characterisation unless one also proves the unreliability of intuitions." (Mihailov, 2016, p. 2). On the observation that post hoc reasoning need not be confabulatory, see also Greenspan, 2015; Sauer, 2012a, 2012b; Schwitzgebel and Ellis, 2017, p. 172.
208 Pollock, 1986.

acter of [the first-order evidence] itself, or about subjects' capacities and dispositions for responding rationally to [the first-order evidence]."[209] Higher-order defeat occurs when the higher-order evidence suggests that the first-order evidence does not support the proposition in the way it had been taken to support it. Higher-order defeat is thus similar to ordinary undercutting defeat in that both involve the severing of the connection between a piece or body of evidence and the proposition it is thought to support. However, higher-order defeat is in an important respect different in that it implies that one's assessment of the first-order evidence was flawed to begin with. As David Christensen points out, defeating higher-order evidence "indicates that my former beliefs were rationally sub-par. This is evidence of my own rational failure."[210] Similarly, Lasonen-Aarnio observes that "defeat by higher-order evidence has a retrospective aspect, providing a subject with evidence that her belief was never rational, reasonable, or justified to start out with."[211] Ordinary undercutting defeaters, by contrast, do not have this implication. While the primary argument, if successful, shows that our automatic, emotion-based intuitions fail to support deontology, it does not imply that it was a mistake to take these intuitions to support deontology before we learned about their dubious origins. The secondary argument, by contrast, relies on evidence to the effect that deontologists' assessment of the first-order evidence was flawed in the first place. Thus, the anti-deontological debunking project does not only involve two complementary debunking arguments but two different *types* of debunking arguments.

The distinction between these two types of debunking arguments is not just academic. As I will explain below in more detail, the second type of debunking argument is open to an objection that the first type of debunking argument is not open to, an objection that tells us something about the nature of debunking arguments and their place in academic debate. This will be the second of two objections that I will raise with regard to the argument from confabulation. The first objection concerns again the limited scope of the argument.

---

209 Kelly, 2014; see also Christensen, 2010; Feldman, 2006.
210 Christensen, 2010, p. 185.
211 Lasonen-Aarnio, 2014, p. 317. Yet another commentator writes that "higher order evidence is evidence that bears on evidential relations, or evidence that bears on what is *rational*." (Schoenfield, 2014, p. 426).

5.3 The scope problem

One objection that we raised against both the argument from evolutionary history and the argument from moral irrelevance was that it targets only a small selection of deontological intuitions. The scope of these attacks on our deontological intuitions was rather circumscribed. A similar objection can be raised against the argument from confabulation. Greene and Singer suggest that deontological theory is merely the product of confabulatory post hoc rationalization. They acknowledge that deontologists engage in calm and dispassionate reasoning, too, but — as Greene writes — "what looks like moral rationalism is actually moral *rationalization*."[212] Now, while Greene and Singer may be right that *some* deontological theories result from confabulatory post hoc rationalization, they can hardly claim to have shown that this applies to all or even the greater part of deontological theories.

To see why, consider that a deontological theory must meet two conditions in order to be a plausible target for the argument from confabulation.

First, the claims of this theory must accord with our intuitive gut reactions. A given deontological theory can only be dismissed as the rationalization of some deontological gut reaction if it confirms this gut reaction. Also, it is precisely the strange coincidence that deontological theorists (allegedly) tend to confirm our intuitive gut reactions that makes the post hoc rationalization hypothesis so compelling in the first place. The observation that deontological theorists tend to find that our pre-reflective intuitions are correct calls for an explanation. And given that post hoc rationalization is a common and well documented phenomenon, the unlikelihood of this coincidence makes post hoc rationalization the best explanation of the 'data'. By contrast, we would have much less reason to suspect post hoc rationalization if the claims of deontological theory were not predicted by our intuitive gut reactions.

Second, as explained above, the intuition that is (allegedly) being rationalized must first have been shown to be off-track. For only then is post hoc reasoning epistemically problematic. Post hoc justification is then very likely to be confabulatory because we are producing a justification for a judgment that there is no reason to assume to be justifiable. By contrast, if the initial intuition is sound, post hoc reasoning need not be confabulatory. This entails that the claims of the deontological theories that are debunked as products of post hoc reasoning must accord with the intuitive gut reactions that are targeted by the primary argument. If these theories are in accord with *other* intuitions, there is less reason to dismiss

---

212 Greene, 2014, p. 718.

them as 'mere rationalizations'. Although they might then be the results of post hoc reasoning, too, these instances of post hoc reasoning could well be perfectly benign.

Each of these two conditions limit the scope of the argument from confabulation. Consider first the requirement that the claims of the deontological theory must confirm our intuitions. Greene and Singer are assuming that this is the case. They point out that there are many sophisticated deontological theories that, surprisingly, just so happen to confirm our gut reactions. And Greene rightly points out that arch-deontologist Immanuel Kant even explicitly admits to being engaged in producing a justification of popular moral lore.[213] But 'deontology' is a fairly heterogenous philosophical school, and not all deontologists converge on the same conclusions. Therefore, they cannot possibly *all* confirm our intuitions. Greene and Singer's argument from confabulation presupposes that the core claims of more elaborate deontological theories are the same, which is patently not the case.

Consider now the condition that the intuitions that are allegedly being rationalized must first have been shown to be unreliable. This requirement means that only a small subset of deontological theories can plausibly be dismissed as results of confabulatory post hoc rationalization. As observed in previous chapters, the scope of the different versions of the primary arguments is fairly circumscribed. The argument from evolutionary history and the argument from moral irrelevance face the scope problem. They debunk only the few deontological intuitions for which an evolutionary explanation has been provided or that have been shown to be responsive to morally irrelevant factors. To the majority of deontological intuitions this does not apply. The functionalist argument does not even seek to debunk all deontological intuitions to begin with, accepting deontological intuitions about familiar, 'Me vs Us' problems as quite reliable. Thus, the different versions of the primary argument target only a small subset of our deontological intuitions, leaving deontological intuitions about a whole range of subject matters completely unscathed. This means that Greene and Singer have no concrete evidence that more elaborate deontological theories about these subject matters may be results of confabulatory post hoc rationalization. For there is no evidence that these theories confirm gut reactions that are known to be unreliable.

To illustrate these two points, consider the problem of distributive justice. First, given that there is an immense variety of non-consequentialist theories about how resources ought to be distributed within a society, they cannot possi-

---

213 Greene, 2008, p. 35.

bly all confirm our intuitive gut reactions regarding distributive justice (whatever these intuitive gut reactions may consist in). As a result, it cannot be the case that all non-consequentialist theories are rationalizations of these intuitive gut reactions of ours. Indeed, some of these theories are arguably quite counterintuitive. A case in point may be libertarian conceptions of distributive justice, which are often dismissed as counterintuitive if not morally repugnant. Few people have libertarian gut reactions.[214] Second, Greene and Singer have so far failed to show that there even is anything wrong with our deontological intuitions about questions of distributive justice. These intuitions have as of yet not been targeted by any version of the primary argument. It may therefore well be the case that our deontological intuitions about these questions are correct. In this case, philosophical efforts to 'rationalize' these intuitions might yield perfectly sound philosophical theories. If what our intuitions tell us is true, attempts to make sense of these truths need not be confabulatory.

Distributive justice is just one of many philosophical issues that do not meet the two conditions. And while intuitions about distributive justice meet neither condition, the argument from confabulation fails as soon as just one of the two conditions is not met. There is thus no basis for dismissing all or even the bulk of deontological theories as products of confabulatory post hoc rationalization.

5.4 Debunking arguments and higher-order evidence

There is another, more fundamental problem with the argument from confabulation, the exploration of which can teach us something important about the structure of philosophical debate and the place of genealogical arguments in it. To dismiss more elaborate deontological theories as just the result of post hoc rationalization is really just a polite way of saying that deontologists are probably bad thinkers, that is, that their claims need not be taken too seriously because they are probably not assessing the evidence correctly anyway. And this blunter formulation of the secondary argument should strike one as objectionable.

However, it is not immediately clear exactly what is objectionable about this way of arguing. One might be tempted to dismiss it as an *ad hominem* fallacy, but this would be wrong.[215] For the argument, although certainly *ad hominem*

---

214 Though maybe they can be brought to have them by reading literature that suggests that libertarianism *is* intuitive (Huemer, 2013).

215 Kumar and Campbell think that the secondary argument involves a genetic fallacy (which may be regarded as a subspecies of *ad hominem* fallacy). They therefore suggest that Greene should say that the intuitions debunked by the primary argument make up the principal evi-

in some sense, is not fallacious. A fallacy is an argument that disguises as a sound argument but really fails to warrant belief in its conclusion.[216] But casting doubt on the merits of some doctrine by showing its proponents to be misjudging the evidence is not fallacious in this sense. The secondary argument is an instance of what Harvey Siegel and John Biro call an argument from lack of authority, which may be viewed as a special type of *ad hominem* argument. When we put forth an argument from lack of authority,

> we attempt to persuade ourselves or our audience that some property of the advocate of a certain claim justifies us in rejecting that advocacy as providing reason for the claim. Again, everything turns – should turn – on the genuineness and relevance of the property in question. When it is really present and when its presence bears on whether the advocacy of the claim by its defender provides warrant for our not believing it, there is nothing wrong with appealing to it. (It is, of course, a mistake to think that doing so is, in and of itself, to provide an argument *for* the denial of the claim. Whatever the rhetorical intentions and consequences, the only conclusion for which one has an argument, strictly speaking, is one against accepting the claim without other grounds being offered.)[217]

The argument from confabulation would be fallacious if it stated that deontology is wrong or that we can be absolutely certain that all elaborate defenses of deontology are results of fallacious post hoc rationalization. For this would be to ignore that this debunking argument can only make an epistemological and probabilistic point. But this is not how the argument should be understood. Greene and Singer do not commit the error of concluding that their debunking argument 'provides an argument for the denial' of deontology, rather than just to defeat the evidence in its favor. And Greene correctly concludes that his argument shows at best that "it is *exceedingly unlikely* that there is any rationally coherent normative moral theory that can accommodate our moral intuitions.

---

dence in support of deontology, which renders the secondary argument obsolete (2012, pp. 313, 327 n7). I disagree on both counts. It strikes me as inaccurate to portray deontology as being mainly justified by appeal to intuitive gut reactions (just think of deontology in the Kantian tradition; see Kauppinen, 2014, p. 297), and the secondary argument is also not fallacious.

216 Or, as Biro and Siegel put it: "An argument is fallacious if it masquerades as being able to yield knowledge or reasonable belief but cannot in fact do so." (2006, p. 2; see also 1992; Hahn and Oaksford, 2006; Siegel and Biro, 1997). This conception of fallacies is not uncontroversial. I am here siding with the proponents of the epistemological account of argumentation (for an instructive overview, see Lumer, 2005).

217 Siegel and Biro, 1997, p. 287. The notion that *ad hominem* arguments and arguments from authority need not be fallacious is by now widely (if not universally) acknowledged, see e.g. Coleman, 1995; Goldman, 1999, pp. 152–152; Hinman, 1982; Johnson, 2009; Korb, 2003; Lumer, 1990, pp. 256–257; Putnam, 2010.

Moreover, anyone who claims to have such a theory, or even part of one, *almost certainly* does not. Instead, what that person *probably* has is a moral rationalization."[218] He does not purport to have conclusively proven that all elaborate defenses of deontology are flawed. So if Greene and Singer are right that deontologists are probably just post hoc rationalizers, the secondary argument, although certainly *ad hominem*, is not an *ad hominem* fallacy.

Rather, the problem with their argument is, I submit, that academic debate is committed to a higher standard of precision. This standard rules out critiques that rely on higher-order evidence, which – while not fallacious – typically yield only an approximate assessment of the first-order evidence. When criticizing some doctrine, one must engage with the first-order evidence that has been adduced in support of this doctrine rather than speculate about what is 'probably' the case. It does not suffice to invoke higher-order evidence to the effect that there is probably no reason to expect the first-order evidence to actually support the doctrine. The argument from confabulation violates this standard. It relies entirely on higher-order evidence and refuses to even consider the arguments that deontologists have appealed to to defend deontology. As a consequence, it yields only an approximate estimate of whether independent arguments for deontology are sound, thereby failing to defeat the evidence in its entirety. It leaves us wondering whether one of the more complex cases for deontology might not be sound after all.

A hint as to why resorting to rough estimates in this way is illegitimate in academic discussions is provided by Christopher Johnson, who, discussing the admissibility of *ad hominem* arguments, remarks:

> Taking as a starting point the idea that we have limited rational capacities, there will be times when we just cannot [...] engag[e] in further investigation or look[...] into the topic ourselves. We may either not have sufficient time to do this – or even if we do we might not be prepared to dedicate that time given other demands we face – or we may not have the necessary intellectual skills or abilities to understand the issues concerned. It may well be in such cases that the reply is made that judgment should thus be suspended; but often decisions are required of us even when we are unable to determine the issue fully factually to our satisfaction. In such cases it seems we have to appeal to criteria other than the facts of the case since those facts are underdetermining. Turning at this point to judging the people who consider the facts can now be a sensible progression.[219]

---

218 Greene, 2008, p. 72, emphasis added. He also admits that his argument "will be speculative and will not be conclusive" (p. 36).

219 Johnson, 2009, p. 257. Similarly, Christoph Lumer points out that such arguments are economical but suboptimal due to their probabilistic nature, and therefore not suitable for scientific inquiry (1990, pp. 248, 256–257).

By contrast, resorting to *ad hominem* arguments in academic debates, as Greene and Singer do, is illegitimate because academic philosophical inquiry does not seem to be subject to the above-mentioned two constraints. Academic philosophical inquiry is typically not subject to time constraints. There is not assumed to be a deadline by which the dispute between deontologists and consequentialists (or, for that matter, between Fregeans and Millians, A-theorists and B-theorists, etc.) has to be resolved. Academic philosophical inquiry is not about making decisions at a certain point in time. Rather, philosophical inquiry is usually conducted *sub specie aeternitatis*. And academic philosophical inquiry is also informed by the tacit assumption that we can ultimately get to the bottom of things if only we try hard enough. Clearly, the way philosophical debates are carried out does not suggest that it is considered pointless to continue exchanging and scrutinizing first-order arguments as this will never lead to success anyway. In a nutshell, the attitude implicit in academic philosophical (and arguably most other academic) inquiry is: 'Let's take our time and figure this out.' Singer and Greene's reasoning violates these assumptions. They jump to premature probabilistic conclusions without there being any need to do so.

The above considerations also help us make sense of what is wrong with arguments that are essentially like Singer and Greene's but even more strikingly inappropriate. Consider the following debunking arguments, which, like Greene and Singer's, rely on higher-order evidence:

(1) This argument for theory *t* is probably flawed because its proponent is just a graduate student from a mediocre university.
(2) This argument for theory *t* is probably flawed because its proponent has always been horribly wrong on these issues in the past.
(3) This solution to the mind-body problem is probably flawed because the human mind tends to be extremely fallible when it comes to solving such intricate philosophical problems as the mind-body problem.

Or, indeed, a deontologist might be tempted to retort:

(4) Integrating philosophy, neuroscience, psychology and evolutionary theory is an extremely tricky and error-prone undertaking. Therefore, Greene and Singer's empirically informed debunking of deontology is very probably flawed.

Finally, to offer a non-philosophical example:

(5) This empirical study that purports to prove claim *c* is probably flawed as its authors are driven by ideological motives and thus biased towards *c*.

While the above arguments need not be fallacious, these and similar arguments are clearly not permitted in academic discussion. The graduate student may rightly insist that he be shown exactly where the flaw in the argument is, and so may the proponents of the second and third argument. And Greene and Singer may of course insist that their argument be taken seriously and carefully examined, rather than dismissed as 'very probably flawed' on such higher-order grounds. And the authors of the empirical study may insist that they be shown exactly what is wrong with the design of their study or with their interpretation of the results. And the reason for this is that we are under no pressure to take such 'shortcuts', which yield only approximate results. We have enough time and cognitive resources at our disposal to evaluate the arguments on the basis of the first-order evidence, making it unnecessary to use rough-and-ready heuristics. By the same token, then, a proponent of a more sophisticated defense of deontology need not accept Greene and Singer's argument from confabulation. When charged with probably just being a post hoc rationalizer, the proponent of a more sophisticated defense of deontology may justly retort: "This is all well and good, but now show me where my argument has gone wrong." In academic philosophical discussion, which it governed by the 'Let's take our time and figure this out' attitude, this proponent of deontology is owed an answer.

Some might want to suggest that we revise our academic practices and jettison the 'Let's take our time and figure this out' attitude in favor of a 'Let's us come to a decision and make a rough estimate' attitude. Indeed, in light of persistent, sometimes centuries-old philosophical peer disagreement, one might feel that there is simply no hope of settling controversial issues in the traditional way by reviewing the first-order evidence. Perhaps we should therefore resort to arguments like that from confabulation or like the ones above in order to come to at least a comparative conclusion, as one may call it. I will not here try to argue against this way of reforming academic philosophical inquiry. Rather, I wish to observe that this would be a revisionary approach, involving a significant departure from the actual academic culture. My claim is therefore a conditional one, whose antecedent I take to be widely affirmed in the current academic culture: If we have enough time and intellectual skills to assess the first-order evidence, it is illegitimate to take argumentative shortcuts that yield only approximate conclusions.[220]

---

220 To be sure, one can think of arguments from higher-order evidence that are not just approximate. For instance, if we *know for sure* that the proponent of some view has taken a drug that makes him *entirely* irrational (that is, he shows no sensitivity to the evidence *whatsoever*), this

I suspect that this maxim underlies much of the skepticism that the genealogical method has attracted, especially from analytic philosophers. But the problem with genealogical arguments that rely on higher-order evidence has often been misdescribed. Recall John Searle's rant against postmodernist writers who dismiss the Western rationalistic tradition as 'phono-phallo-logocentric'. Searle accuses these writers of committing the *genetic fallacy* and the *ad hominem* fallacy. But as we have seen, to argue that some doctrine ought to be distrusted because it reflects intellectual bias or ideology is not fallacious *per se*. Rather, an argumentative strategy of this kind is objectionable because it tends to be unnecessarily imprecise and speculative. Without reasonable excuse, it fails to actually engage with the (say) phallocentric reasoning and to specify where exactly it goes wrong. As a result, it leaves us wondering whether it might not be correct after all.

Fortunately, all this does not mean that evidence of cognitive malfunctions on the part of the proponents of a given philosophical theory must entirely go to waste. There are still various ways in which one may fruitfully make use of such information.

First, arguments from higher-order evidence may be admissible in other contexts. I have been concerned with academic discussions as carried out in academic books, journals and at conferences. If a deontologist were to submit an academic article arguing along the lines of (4), it would rightly be rejected as too conjectural. But this ban on a certain type of argument does not necessarily apply in other contexts, such as, say, informal chats between colleagues. In particular, it does not apply in contexts in which intellectual resources are limited and/or there is an urgent need to arrive at a decision. For instance, debunking arguments based on higher-order evidence are suitable for private use, so to speak. As private individuals, we cannot hope to sort out every philosophical question by exhaustively sifting through the first-order evidence. This makes resorting to rough estimates based on higher-order evidence legitimate. Thus, while we are not allowed to dismiss deontological theory as probably just confabulatory in an official academic debate, it is unobjectionable to do so 'in private'. Likewise, it is permissible to argue from higher-order evidence in those real-life situations in which we must make a quick decision. If the trolley is hurtling down the track towards the immobilized workers, and a group of people has just a few minutes to decide what to do, advancing the argument from confabulation would be perfectly legitimate. Or, to give a more realistic example, the

---

would arguably suffice to dismiss whatever argument he puts forth on the grounds that he is under the influence of this drug. But typically, arguments from higher-order evidence are weaker in that they only establish that the proponent of the to-be-debunked view is *probably* not responding to the evidence.

deliberative process of experts – philosophical or otherwise – who sit on panels that decide about pressing issues of public import should not be subject to the above constraints.[221]

Second, one may make use of such higher-order evidence without actually mentioning it in one's argument. Such evidence may yield useful hints and thus *guide* one in one's inquiry. If you possess, say, evidence to the effect that deontological moral theory is just the product of erroneous post hoc rationalization, this would be a good reason to embark on a research project showing that deontologists got it wrong. After all, you already possess higher-order evidence to the effect that deontological arguments are probably flawed. You just need to find these flaws. The prospects of success are therefore exceptionally good. I am not, of course, suggesting that higher-order evidence may absolve one from the duty of being sensitive to the (first-order) evidence and of eventually going where the argument leads. But we can use such evidence as an indicator of which philosophical project may turn out successful. I take it that academic philosophical inquiry is often at least partly guided by higher-order considerations of this kind, and this strikes me as unobjectionable.

Third, there is nothing objectionable about offering debunking explanations that rely on higher-order evidence in addition to one's regular argument as long as they have a purely diagnostic or explanatory rather than argumentative function. After having argued for some doctrine on the basis of regular first-order evidence, one may offer conjectures as to why people have failed to recognize the truth of this doctrine. In most cases, this explanation of people's errors will be trivial and not worth mentioning. Typically, the reason why people fail to notice that a given body of evidence supports a certain conclusion is simply that the human mind is fallible when it comes to solving complex philosophical problems, which is not particularly noteworthy. In some cases, however, the explanation is more interesting and worth exploring. The explanation may be that opponents of the argued-for position are systematically biased or under some kind of ideological delusion, and exposing such biases may be quite instructive and enlightening in its own right. If Greene and Singer are right, there is a systematic bias towards deontology because philosophers tend to post hoc rationalize innate deontological gut reactions. So instead of debunking elaborate defenses of deontology by appeal to higher-order evidence, Greene and Singer could have refuted them in the standard way (that is, by engaging with the first-

---

221 There are of course many other contexts of argumentation that might be worth looking into. Think, for instance, of the political arena or the courtroom. It would be interesting to examine the admissibility of debunking arguments that are based on higher-order evidence in these other contexts, too.

order evidence) and then offered this psychological debunking explanation as a genealogical diagnosis of why philosophers have produced these flawed deontological arguments, as an instructive but dispensable add-on, so to speak. As anticipated in the introduction, this is how Jason Brennan and Peter Jaworski proceed in their defense of markets against critics of commodification. They first present regular, first-order level arguments against the view that some goods should not be for sale. Then, in a second step, they conjecture that anti-commodificationists are merely rationalizing a feeling of disgust that overcomes them at the thought of markets in such goods as sex, organs or surrogacy. That is, rather than to argue from higher-order evidence, they offer evidence of biases on the part of their philosophical opponents as a *diagnosis* of why they were wrong about the moral permissibility of the commodification of certain goods.[222]

It need not necessarily be clear which type of defeating mechanism a given debunking argument relies upon. While the structure of Greene and Singer's anti-deontological debunking arguments is relatively clear, other debunking arguments may be less explicit about their exact mode of operation. Debunkers typically proceed by showing that the cognition of those who hold the to-be-debunked belief is in some way or another flawed. But such cognitive flaws can often manifest themselves in either (or indeed both) of the two above described ways. They can create false impressions of evidence, e. g. by distorting our moral intuitions, and they may lead one to misjudge the available evidence. Arguments of the form 'You just believe that because...' are often indeterminate in this respect. For instance, a leftist critique of some normative political view as 'ideological', as merely reflecting social power relations, may be indeterminate as to whether these power relations have corrupted people's moral intuitions or whether they have led to flawed assessments of the evidence. The same may be true, for instance, of dismissals of egalitarian redistribution as envy-driven, which are popular in libertarian circles.[223] If, as I have argued, one of these two types of debunking arguments is objectionably sloppy, it is important to be precise about which of the two debunking mechanisms a given debunking argument purports to employ.

---

222 Brennan and Jaworski, 2015, p. 1077; 2016, pp. 217–219. One difference, however, is that Greene and Singer have stronger independent evidence of post hoc rationalization on the part of their opponents. Brennan and Jaworski's hypothesis that anti-commodificationists are post hoc rationalizers is at least in part motivated and made plausible by the fact that anti-commodificationist arguments were found to be unconvincing. Greene and Singer's hypothesis that deontologists are post hoc rationalizers, by contrast, is independently motivated.
223 Most prominently Hayek, 1976, p. 98; 2006, pp. 81–82.

5.5 Conclusion

This concludes the investigation of the prospects of the anti-deontological debunking project. While its proponents deserve credit for their methodological ingenuity, the approach they have taken is unlikely to settle the deontology/utilitarianism controversy in the latter's favor. Two principal problems with the debunking project turned out to be its limited scope and the backfiring problem. Not only does it target only a small subset of deontological intuitions. The methods used can be turned against utilitarianism, too. The functionalist argument runs into its own substantial and methodological problems.

The discussion has yielded two more general takeaways. One is that the value of experimental findings regarding people's sensitivity to morally irrelevant factors remains somewhat elusive. It still remains to be seen how such findings, and arguments from moral irrelevance based on them, allow us to make significant methodological progress.

Another general takeaway concerns the argumentation-theoretical nature of debunking arguments and their status within academic debate. Contrary to conventional wisdom, genealogical arguments are not fallacious. But once we distinguish between debunking arguments that rely on ordinary undercutting defeat and those that use higher-order defeat, we can make sense of the widespread sense that there is something objectionable about genealogical arguments. Debunking arguments that rely on higher-order defeat are objectionably sloppy and therefore, while not fallacious, should not be used in an academic setting.

6 Realism, Constructivism, and Evolution

6.1 Introduction

The preceding discussion has revealed problems with local evolutionary debunking arguments, that is, with debunking arguments that seek to undermine a relatively small and specific set of moral beliefs. Foremost among these problems was the backfiring problem. Local debunking arguments are difficult to control in the sense that they have more far-reaching skeptical implications than intended. Evolutionary debunking arguments are too destructive and uncontrollable to lend themselves to high-precision attacks on circumscribed positions within normative ethics, such as deontology.

One possible response to this problem is to embrace it by constructing a global rather than a local evolutionary debunking argument. Rather than to target a precisely circumscribed set of moral beliefs, such as all deontological but no consequentialist ones, one might maintain that evolution has had a more extensive and indiscriminate impact on our moral beliefs. Such a more sweeping, global, evolutionary debunking argument has been put forth by Sharon Street.[224] As examples of beliefs that can readily be explained in evolutionary terms, Street cites such convictions as that one's own survival is good, that we have special obligations to our relatives, especially our children, and that one ought to reciprocate cooperative behavior and punish defective behavior.[225] But she takes it that virtually all of our evaluative beliefs are eventually affected by evolutionary debunking.[226] Street does not assume that each and every evaluative belief of ours has been shaped by evolutionary forces. But she reckons that evolution's influence has been sufficiently thoroughgoing as to 'contaminate' our entire web of evaluative beliefs:

> [I]f the fund of evaluative judgements with which human reflection began was thoroughly contaminated with illegitimate influence [...] then the tools of rational reflection were equally contaminated, for the latter are always just a subset of the former. It follows that all our reflection over the ages has really just been a process of assessing evaluative judgements that are mostly off the mark in terms of others that are mostly off the mark."[227]

---

224 Street, 2006
225 Street, 2006, p. 115.
226 The terms 'evaluative' and 'normative' are sometimes used to refer to axiological and deontic properties, respectively. Here, these terms are used more loosely.
227 Street, 2006, p. 124.

https://doi.org/10.1515/9783110750195-007

One might retort that not all evaluative judgements have been influenced by evolutionary forces to the same extent. Indeed, I have myself suggested above that there are deontological intuitions that do not seem amenable to an evolutionary debunking explanation in any obvious way. For the sake of argument, however, I will in this chapter go along with Street's assumption that evolutionary forces have had a global impact on our evaluative judgments.

While Greene and Singer sought to refute deontology and to defend utilitarianism, Street has metaethical ambitions. Her target is realism, the view that evaluative facts are attitude-independent, and her aim is to establish constructivism, the anti-realist view that all evaluative facts are constructed by our attitudes. According to Street, the evolutionary origins of our evaluative beliefs pose a dilemma for realists: either, on the first horn of the dilemma, we assume that there is no relation whatsoever between the evaluative truth and the direction in which evolutionary pressures have pushed our evaluative beliefs. In this case, it would be an incredible coincidence if our evaluative beliefs turned out to be even roughly correct. Or, on the second horn, we posit a tracking-relation between the evaluative truth and the forces of evolution. We assume that we have evolved to track the evaluative truth because the capacity to discern evaluative truths was adaptive. But the tracking-account is dismissed by Street as scientifically untenable. This leaves realists with the first horn of the dilemma, which entails radical evaluative skepticism.[228] Constructivists, by contrast, do not face this dilemma. Unlike realists, they can plausibly posit a relation between the evaluative truth and the direction in which evolutionary forces have pushed our evaluative judgments, as the evaluative truth is, on the constructivist view, determined by our evaluative attitudes. Given the implausibility of radical evaluative skepticism, Street takes this Darwinian Dilemma for realism to establish constructivism: "our response must be to adjust our metaethical view so as to become antirealists."[229]

Street herself advocates a brand of constructivism that she has referred to as Humean constructivism. According to Humean constructivism, our reasons for action are more or less directly a function of what we judge to be our reasons for action. A person has reason to perform some action if her judgment to perform this action coheres with her other evaluative judgments, or – as Street puts it – if this judgment "withstands scrutiny from the standpoint of [her]

---

228 Street, 2006, pp. 121–135
229 Street, 2006, p. 141; see also 2015, 2016.

other judgments about reasons."[230] Humean constructivism is Humean in that it denies that this entails any categorical reasons for action, that it, reasons that everybody has irrespective of their contingent ends or evaluative attitudes. It contrasts with Kantian versions of constructivism, as championed for instance by Christine Korsgaard and Michael Smith, according to which at least some substantive normative conclusions follow from within every agent's practical stance.[231] Street is skeptical about the prospects of deriving categorical normativity from within a constructivist framework.[232] Her endorsement of Humean constructivism is based primarily on the conjunction of the Darwinian argument and her rejection of Kantian versions of constructivism.[233]

In this chapter, I will pick up the 'backfiring' theme from the previous chapters and show that the Darwinian argument for Humean constructivism backfires, too, albeit in a slightly different way.

Street's debunking project is structurally different from other debunking arguments. Typically, a debunking argument seeks to undermine some belief or doctrine by providing a debunking explanation of why people have come to accept the targeted belief or doctrine. Street, by contrast, does not provide a debunking explanation of why people have come to accept realism (the targeted doctrine). Instead, she argues that we should abandon realism because realism exposes our evaluative beliefs to evolutionary debunking arguments. Strictly speaking, she does not debunk realism, but offers an argument against realism that *involves* a debunking argument. Reflecting this difference, the backfiring problem for Street's evolutionary argument for Humean constructivism is not that there is an evolutionary explanation of people's belief in Humean constructivism (which would not be particularly plausible to begin with).[234] Rather, the argument backfires in that, upon closer inspection, it calls not for a conversion to (Humean) constructivism but, in fact, to what I will call skepticism about morality. Again, a debunking project turns out to have much more skeptical implications than intended by its author and to fail to achieve its dialectical aim. While much of the literature that Street's argument has generated has focused

---

230 Street, 2016, p. 306; see also 2008a, 2012, 2016. Street's theory is not the only one that lays claim to the label of 'Humean constructivism'. For a different 'Humean constructivism' with an expressivist and contractualist bent, refer to Lenman, 2010.
231 Street, 2008a, pp. 244–245; 2010, 2012, 2016; see Korsgaard, 1996; Smith, 1994.
232 See in particular Street, 2012.
233 I say ‚primarily', because she also sketches a constitutivist argument for constructivism, to which I return later.
234 Berker develops an argument along these lines (2014, pp. 236–244).

on refuting the epistemological challenge to realism, the focus of this chapter will thus be different. The focus is less on the critical aspect of her argument, her epistemological challenge to realism, and more on the implications of this challenge.[235]

I will begin with some preliminary observations, drawing attention to three tensions in the Darwinian argument for constructivism that are easy to overlook but that have important dialectical implications. One of these tensions is that the argument is ambiguous between two different interpretations, which I will refer to as the epistemological and the normative argument. I will then explain how both of these arguments backfires by supporting skepticism about morality rather than Humean constructivism.

6.2 The Darwinian case against realism and for constructivism

The first of the three preliminary points concerns the scope of evaluative beliefs that are targeted by the debunking argument. At times, Street appears to suggest that *all* evaluative beliefs are debunked if we assume a realist framework. She asserts that realists must accept that they are "in all likelihood hopeless at grasping the normative truth", and she speaks of *"global evaluative skepticism* in the sense of a conviction that one has no idea how to live."[236] But these statements are at odds with how she actually defines realism, namely as the view that "there are at least *some* evaluative facts or truths that hold independently of all our evaluative attitudes."[237] And she explicitly concedes that "[w]e all hold a mind-dependent view of *some* kinds of value".[238] The targeted view, 'realism', is thus not the view that no evaluative facts are attitude-dependent, but the view that some evaluative facts are attitude-independent. Street is right to propose this somewhat more cautious definition of realism, as most paradigmatic realists are realists only with regard to a subset of the evaluative domain, in particular morality, while accepting that other evaluative facts, e.g. facts about a

---

235 For some attempts to defuse the challenge, see Brosnan, 2011; Copp, 2008; Enoch, 2010; Hanson, 2017; Huemer, 2008; Schafer, 2010; Shafer-Landau, 2012; Skarsaune, 2011; Wielenberg, 2010.

236 Street, 2016, p. 326 and 2015, p. 691. She also writes that "[a]ccepting this radical skeptical conclusion would involve nothing less than suspending *all* evaluative judgment." (2015, p. 692).

237 Street, 2016, p. 295, emphasis added, see also 2008b, p. 218; 2015, p. 690.

238 Street, 2015, p. 690. Although this may be an overstatement. Parfit, for one, is arguably a global realist (2011a).

person's non-moral good, are attitude-dependent. I therefore assume, along with many other commentators, that we are in the first instance concerned with *moral* facts, that is, with whether *moral facts* should be understood to be attitude-dependent or attitude-independent.[239] If Street is correct, 'realism' would entail *moral* skepticism, but not necessarily global evaluative skepticism.

Second, as already noted, Street's argument is ambiguous between two different readings. Her argument is a *reductio* that can be interpreted in two different ways, yielding two different arguments that differ with respect to the implication of realism that is deemed 'absurd'. According to the epistemological argument, realism must be rejected because it implies the indiscernibility of the moral truth. This version of the argument is premised on the assumption that the moral truth must in principle be discernible, whatever this truth may turn out to consist in. Accepting that we are hopeless at discovering the moral truth would mean that we "will be paralyzed and unable to proceed with normative reasoning"[240], which Street thinks is not an option: "one *must* reject this conclusion if one is to go on making normative judgments at all."[241] For this argument to work, it is necessary that realism does not just imply that our current moral beliefs are very likely mistaken, but also that there is no way of discovering the moral truth in the future. I will refer to the view that there are objective moral facts that we will never be able to discern as 'pessimistic skeptical realism'. The slightly more optimistic position that there are objective moral facts, that our current moral beliefs about them are unjustified, but that it is possible to discern them in the future, will be referred to as 'optimistic skeptical realism'. Optimistic skeptical realism does not entail permanent practical paralysis, as it leaves open the possibility of overcoming the paralysis by acquiring justified moral beliefs in the future. Permanent practical paralysis follows only if, as Street believes, "we are in all likelihood hopeless at *discovering* the normative truth."[242] The epistemological argument rests on the assumption that realists are forced to accept pessimistic skeptical realism.

According to the normative argument, realism must be rejected in favor of constructivism because realism implies that our current moral beliefs are most likely wrong. The normative argument is premised on the assumption that it is "implausible" that our "normative views are in all likelihood mistaken".[243] Sure-

---

239 See Brosnan, 2011; Copp, 2008; Graber, 2012; Hopster, 2018; Joyce, 2013c; Klenk, 2017; Shafer-Landau, 2012, to name but a few.
240 Street, 2016, p. 330; see also 2015, p. 692.
241 Street, 2016, p. 330.
242 Street, 2016, p. 330, emphasis added.
243 Street, 2016, p. 313.

ly, we may safely assume that "many of our normative judgments are true."[244] But this assumption is incompatible with realism, which entails that even our most central evaluative beliefs – "that we should care for our children, that altruism is admirable while cheating is to be condemned"[245], and so forth – are very likely false. By contrast, constructivism "preserves many of our evaluative views – allowing us to see why we are reasonably reliable about matters of value – while at the same time allowing us to see ourselves as evolved creatures."[246] The normative argument requires only that the realist framework entails optimistic skeptical realism. It does not require that realism entails the indiscernibility of moral facts (pessimistic skeptical realism).[247]

The Epistemological Argument

P_E1) Of the relevant metaethical options, we should adopt the most plausible metaethical theory that does not entail practical paralysis.

P_E2) Given the evolutionary origins of our moral beliefs, holding on to the realist framework would entail the indiscernibility of the moral truth and permanent practical paralysis (pessimistic moral realism).

P_E3) Humean constructivism does not entail the indiscernibility of the moral truth and practical paralysis.

P_E4) Realism and Humean constructivism are the two relevant options.

C_E) We should adopt Humean constructivism

The Normative Argument

P_N1) Of the relevant metaethical options, we should adopt the most plausible metaethical theory that entails little moral revisionism.

P_N2) Given the evolutionary origins of our moral beliefs, holding on to the realist framework would entail that our current moral beliefs are probably, if corrigibly, mistaken (optimistic moral realism).

P_N3) Humean constructivism entails little moral revisionism.

P_N4) Realism and Humean constructivism are the two relevant options.

C_N) We should adopt Humean constructivism.

---

244 Street, 2016, p. 305.
245 Street, 2015, p. 693.
246 Street, 2015, p. 693.
247 A version of the normative argument is discussed by Risberg and Tersman (2020, pp. 289–290).

These are the two versions of Street's argument that I engage with below.

Third, we must be careful in characterizing the view that Street seeks to establish. Street suggests that we abandon belief in attitude-independent evaluative facts and instead adopt the view that all evaluative facts are grounded in our evaluative attitudes. But it is important to see that one can reach this conclusion via two different routes. One route is by concluding that the evaluative facts that we had taken to be attitude-independent – e.g. that cheating is to be condemned – are really attitude-dependent. This would mean that our current moral beliefs are by and large correct but that we were mistaken about *why* these moral facts obtain. The fact that cheating is to be condemned is not attitude-independent but constituted by our evaluative judgments. The other route would be by concluding that the entire domain of moral discourse is fundamentally confused. That is, we might conclude that the relevant beliefs – that cheating is to be condemned, etc. – are probably altogether mistaken because they are about facts that do not even exist. Other domains of evaluative discourse, by contrast, which are about attitude-dependent (e.g. prudential) facts, would not be fundamentally erroneous in this way. This is the view that, for lack a better term, I refer to as 'skepticism about morality'. Skepticism about morality states that we are not *justified* to believe in such facts or that there are *probably* no such facts. Unlike moral error theory, it does not conclusively rule out their existence. Debunking arguments are too weak to establish such more radical conclusions. Resting on undercutting defeat, they only undermine the justification of a belief, but they do not provide evidence for the falsity of the belief.

Both views are examples of global anti-realism, as neither view posits the existence of attitude-independent evaluative facts. But in one case (if we become constructivists), global anti-realism follows from the anti-realist re-construal of a set of evaluative facts (moral facts) that had previously been taken to be attitude-independent. In the other case (if we accept skepticism about morality), global anti-realism results from excising and jettisoning the domain of evaluative discourse that is attitude-independent (morality), so that only attitude-dependent evaluative facts remain. The former conversion to anti-realism is, at least on the surface, relatively conservative, whereas the latter is skeptical with regard to an entire domain of evaluative discourse. Compare this to how a theist might come to espouse the view that everything that exists is natural and that there exist no supernatural entities. One option is to conclude that everything divine is really natural rather than supernatural, which would allow the theist to retain most of her religious beliefs, at least superficially. The other option is to conclude that there are no gods, which would render her religious beliefs false. Both are versions of global naturalism. The former is entailed by a naturalistic re-construal of 'god facts', whereas the latter is entailed by the denial of there being any gods.

Street must be understood as proposing the former approach and as rejecting the latter. Her view is that our moral beliefs are mostly true but that we have been mistaken about what makes them true. She is adamant that Humean constructivism "allows us to say almost everything we ever were inclined to say about people's reasons, with the exception of a swath of extremely strong realist claims."[248] Indeed, according to the normative argument, it is precisely because Humean constructivism confirms the larger part of our current moral beliefs that we should convert to it. Skepticism about morality, by contrast, implies, like realism, that our current moral beliefs are unjustified, a possibility that Street thinks must be avoided.[249]

I belabor this point because it has an important dialectical implication. It means that skepticism about morality, although an anti-realist view (if combined with an attitude-dependent account of non-moral facts), is an *alternative* view to the one defended by Street. Contrary to P_E4 and P_N4, there is a third relevant option, skepticism about morality, which Street fails to take seriously. P_E4 and P_N4 suggest that we must choose between sticking with the realist framework – which would mean accepting pessimistic or optimistic skeptical realism, respectively – or Humean constructivism. But instead of accepting pessimistic or optimistic skeptical realism, we might as well become skeptics about morality. The availability of skepticism about morality as a third option is relevant because skepticism about morality is more plausible an alternative to Humean constructivism than (optimistic or pessimistic skeptical) realism. If we start with a realist conception of morality and learn that each of our moral judgments is unjustified, there is something strange about insisting that there must be moral facts all the same, which may or may not be discernible. It is much more natural to conclude that there probably simply are no moral facts to begin with, that is, to accept skepticism about morality.[250] The view that there are moral facts that we have failed to correctly identify should only be considered when there is some independent rationale for assuming the existence of such facts. But it is difficult to image what this rationale might be. It would be odd to assume that there *have to be* moral facts.[251]

---

248 Street, 2016, p. 328.
249 This is in line with Ronald Dworkin's rejection of error theory (1996, pp. 113–116).
250 For a similar observation, see Tropman, 2013, p. 135.
251 Enoch's argument from deliberative dispensability (2007) might come close to offering such a rationale. But his argument is specifically an argument for positing attitude-*independent* normative facts. If it is sound, the existence of attitude-independent normative facts has successful-

For illustration, consider again religious belief: imagine you are an ancient Greek believing in the traditional Greek gods (Zeus, Athena, Artemis, etc.). Now assume that your beliefs about each of these gods have been debunked. Surely, what you should conclude is that there probably are no gods to begin with, rather than that you have merely been mistaken about *who* the gods are. You should draw the latter conclusion only if you have independent reason to believe in the existence of any gods, say, because their existence is necessary to explain certain natural phenomena.

As Street presents it, her case for Humean constructivism rests on the assumption that realists must accept optimistic or pessimistic skeptical realism. She then suggests that constructivism is more plausible than optimistic or pessimistic skeptical realism. What I have suggested, however, is that in response to the Darwinian challenge realists, lacking an independent rationale to posit objective moral facts, would be more inclined to accept skepticism about morality than optimistic or pessimistic skeptical realism, even though this involves giving up on realism. Therefore, for the Darwinian argument for constructivism to succeed, it must show that Humean constructivism is superior to skepticism about morality. I will suggest that the opposite is the case. The most natural response is to become skeptics about morality rather than Humean constructivists. Instead, then, of defending realism, I will argue that the Darwinian Dilemma backfires by providing an argument for skepticism about morality rather than Humean constructivism.

6.3 Two arguments and the backfiring problem

The epistemological argument

As we have seen, it is natural to interpret Street as rejecting realism on the grounds that it renders the moral truth indiscernible and thereby practical deliberation impossible. This is what I have dubbed the epistemological argument. It may be worth noting, though, that this epistemological reading of the argument does not conform to the methodological approach that Street officially purports to be pursuing. Following the lead of Ronald Dworkin, Street suggests that metaethical disputes be settled on normative grounds:

---

ly been established, contrary to what Street's Darwinian argument intends to achieve. For a compelling and more in-depth argument that there is no independent rationale for positing objective moral facts, see Tersman, 2019.

> Since we are understanding the realism/antirealism debate as a normative debate like any other — just taking place at a higher level of abstraction than usual — ultimately the argumentative situation here is no different from any other case in which we find two or more of our normative convictions in tension — for instance, when we notice that the principle 'One should always save the greatest number' is in tension with the view that 'One should not sacrifice an innocent to harvest his organs for use by others.' Just as in this organ case we can do nothing but opt for that conviction which, on reflection, seems most plausible all things considered, so I agree we can do nothing in the realism/antirealism debate but opt for the conviction which, on reflection, seems most plausible all things considered.[252]

The epistemological argument, however, is not a normative solution to the metaethical problem, as it is about the in-principle discernibility of the moral truth rather than about the correctness of *specific* moral beliefs. The premise that practical paralysis must be avoided (P_E1) is not a normative premise in the way that '(we are justified to believe that) one should not sacrifice an innocent to harvest his organs for use by others' or '(we are justified to believe that) cheating is to be condemned' are.

The principal problem with the epistemological argument, however, is related to the fact that Street does not take seriously the option of skepticism about morality. According to the epistemological argument, the prospect of 'practical paralysis' must be avoided. *This* is why we must reject realism and become constructivists. But this argument is a non-starter if we take into account that, if we start from a realist conception of morality, the most natural response to the Darwinian challenge is skepticism about morality rather than optimistic or pessimistic skeptical realism. Once all our moral beliefs have been debunked, we should conclude that there probably are no moral facts in the first place. And once we accept skepticism about morality, we do not face the problem of the indiscernibility of the moral truth, as we would not assume there to be any moral facts to begin with. By implication, we would not be 'paralyzed and unable to proceed with normative reasoning'. All the remaining evaluative facts – especially prudential ones – would be tied to our evaluative attitudes and (by Street's own lights) be more or less readily discernible. The epistemological argument thus fails to explain why we must embrace Humean constructivism. Practical paralysis follows only if there is an independent rationale to posit moral facts after all particular moral beliefs have been debunked. But it is unclear what this rationale might be.

The epistemological argument fails because it is ineffective against skepticism about morality. Skepticism about morality does not entail practical paraly-

---

252 Street, 2016, p. 326; see Dworkin, 1996; Kramer, 2009.

sis because it eliminates morality altogether rather than to posit moral facts that we are unable to discern. And skepticism about morality is the most natural response to Street's challenge. Contrary, then, to its intended purpose, this version of the Darwinian challenge supports skepticism about morality rather than Humean constructivism.

The normative argument

According to the second interpretation of Street's argument, we should reject realism because it implies that many of our most deeply held moral beliefs are in all likelihood false. We should instead embrace Humean constructivism, which preserves the bulk of our moral beliefs. The normative argument fits better with Street's suggestion to treat the realism/anti-realism debate as a substantively normative one. It is premised on the normative assumption that it would be implausible if our current moral beliefs were probably mistaken. Street makes the case for constructivism on the grounds that it possesses greater normative plausibility than realism. Although her argument can rightly be called a normative argument, it should be noted that the normative premise (P_N1) should be read as involving an epistemological aspect, too. The assumption is that our moral beliefs are by and large *justified* or *likely to be true*. Realism entails, according to Street, that these beliefs are unjustified or very unlikely to be true. Realism does not entail that these beliefs are actually false, for they might still be true by coincidence. Although Street claims to be "[w]orking from normative premises"[253], she cannot be (and should not be read as) working directly from plain normative premises such as 'cheating is to be condemned'. For realism does not strictly entail their falsity. She must object to realism on the grounds that it renders such beliefs unjustified or very unlikely to be true rather than that it renders them false.

The reason why the normative argument is unconvincing is that Humean constructivism is normatively less appealing than Street has us believe. Street thinks that switching to constructivism 'allows us to say almost everything we were ever inclined to say about people's reasons, with the exception of a swath of extremely strong realist claims'. But Humean constructivism is much more revisionary than Street admits. Its revisionary nature again makes the overlooked third option, skepticism about morality, appear more plausible in comparison.

---

253 Street, 2016, p. 299.

One problem with her normative defence of Humean constructivism concerns this 'swath of extremely strong realist claims' that Street concedes must be abandoned. Realists claim that there are some things that everybody has reason to do or to abstain from doing, irrespective of their contingent attitudes. Humean constructivism denies that this is the case, because it denies that any categorical reasons can be derived from within an attitude-dependent framework. Street maintains that Humean constructivism generally yields fairly intuitive normative results, but she admits that it implies that "[s]ome conceivable agents have reason to exterminate an ethnic group or enslave a race or torture a young child for fun in front of its captive mother."[254] Similarly, Street observes that there may be agents who have most reason to starve themselves to death for the sake of a trim figure or to prefer excruciating pain on a future Tuesday over minor pain on any other day of the week. Humean constructivism allows, in theory, the existence of what Street calls ideally coherent eccentrics: agents whose extremely eccentric value judgments are in equilibrium and therefore correct according to the standards of Humean constructivism. This implication of Humean constructivism strikes many as extremely counterintuitive. Many will pre-theoretically feel that *everyone* has a strong reason to refrain from enslaving a race or from starving themselves to death, no matter what. Street puts a lot of effort into dispelling this impression of counterintuitiveness. Her main line of response is that we must realize how utterly extraordinary these ideally coherent eccentrics are. No real-life person is even remotely similar to an ideally coherent eccentric. Real-life people might hold eccentric evaluative beliefs, but these beliefs disappear once their judgments are made coherent. Given how queer ideally coherent eccentrics are, it is no surprise that we initially find it hard to believe that some beings may have most reason to enslave a race or starve themselves to death. But once we make an effort to vividly imagine what the mindset of such an ideally coherent eccentric would have to look like, it is starting to appear more plausible that they may have overriding reason to do something extremely immoral or self-damaging.[255]

Street's reasoning is certainly not implausible. But the cases that Street discusses in detail, the anorexia case and the future Tuesday indifference case, are concerned with a person's non-moral good. When she turns to the moral case, that of evil Caligula, she offers rather little in the way of argument or illustration. As Street admits, she merely states her conclusions rather than to actually argue for them: "I'll merely state baldly, without arguing for, the additional lessons

---

254 Street, 2016, p. 326.
255 See in particular Street, 2009, 2016.

about [ideally coherent eccentrics] that I think would emerge from a careful consideration of an ideally coherent Caligula."[256] But this comes close to begging the question, as the moral case is the dialectically decisive one. As noted at the outset, even many realists are happy to admit that some evaluative facts, such as a person's non-moral good, are attitude-dependent and non-categorical. The test case are moral facts. Street must show that *they* might plausibly be attitude-dependent and non-categorical, which is a much more difficult task. The implication that some conceivable agent may have most reason to commit terrible atrocities is much more difficult to accept than that her personal good may turn out to be extremely idiosyncratic. It remains unclear to what extent her argument carries over from non-moral to moral questions. If it is true that one cannot derive categorical reasons from within a constructivist framework, constructivism may be a lot less normatively plausible than Street is prepared to concede.

The second and, to my mind, more serious problem is that normative plausibility is not only a question of extensional adequacy. We also hold evaluative beliefs about how evaluative facts are grounded, that is, about in virtue of what certain evaluative facts obtain. Even if Humean constructivism should make intuitively plausible claims about which reasons for action people have, thereby guaranteeing extensional adequacy, it may still make normatively implausible claims about *in virtue of what* these evaluative facts obtain. It may offer a false account of which properties are normatively significant. To be sure, these two aspects are not unrelated. The extension of people's reasons for action depends on how they are grounded. If all evaluative properties are grounded in, say, people's evaluative attitudes, this may have substantive implications about what reasons for action people have. But we should be careful to distinguish these two aspects. Indeed, it is conceivable that two moral theories – one constructivist and one realist – are extensionally indistinguishable while making quite dissimilar grounding claims.[257] And although extensionally indistinguishable, these theories would still differ with regard to their grounding claims and may be found plausible or implausible precisely because of the grounding claims they make. Thus, even if the shift from realism to constructivism might allow us to retain many of our beliefs about what people have reason to do, it will seriously upset our beliefs about *why* people have these reasons.

Consider the problem of abortion. As Enoch points out, when one disagrees with others about the moral status of abortion, if feels like one is disagreeing

---

256 Street, 2009, p. 292.
257 For instance, it is conceivable that the constructivist theories of Michael Smith or Thomas Scanlon yield results that coincide with those of some garden-variety realist theory.

about an attitude-independent matter of fact: "It is in no way like disagreeing over the merits of different kinds of chocolate", which is an attitude-dependent matter. Likewise, when one deliberates about the moral permissibility of abortion, the deliberation does not turn around one's attitudes or preferences. It is directed at facts that transcend one's attitudes.[258] What this indicates is that we do not take our contingent attitudes to be the features that make abortion or other morally relevant actions right or wrong. While people disagree about exactly what these features are, there is a strong intuition that the moral facts are not simply fixed by our attitudes. Our evaluative attitudes just do not seem to be the sort of facts that are relevant when it comes to deciding about normative questions of this sort. This strong and commonsensical intuition is arguably the primary motivation for moral realism in the first place. And it means that switching to constructivism *does* imply changing our most basic evaluative convictions, albeit convictions about which facts matter normatively. Street's contention that switching to constructivism allows us to say most of what we were ever inclined to say about people's reasons ignores the fact that there are important things we want to say (or, for that matter, do *not* want say) about *why* people have the reasons they have. The shift to constructivism leaves at best the façade of our moral belief system intact while it forces us to adopt a revisionary theory about what is behind this façade.

We must not underestimate the significance of what is behind the façade. Consider what one might call Great Books Theory (GBT). According to GBT, the moral facts are determined by a selection of widely approved philosophical books. Facts about justice are determined by John Rawls' *A Theory of Justice*, facts about morality are determined by Tim Scanlon's *What We Owe To Each Other*, and so on. Moral facts are book-dependent, so to speak. Naturally, GBT yields claims about what we ought and ought not do that will strike many as quite reasonable. It might even do better in this respect than Humean constructivism. And yet there is no doubt that overall GBT is an utterly implausible theory. This is because of the absurdity of the claim that the moral truth is determined by what it says in certain books. While many will find it plausible that we should redistribute wealth and secure basic rights and that there should be limits to interpersonal moral aggregation, nobody would want to say that these facts obtain *because* Rawls and Scanlon say so. Mere extensional adequacy is clearly not enough for a theory to be normatively appealing.

Street could concede all of the above but then insist that Humean constructivism is still *more* normatively plausible than skepticism about morality, the

---

258 Enoch, 2014, pp. 195–196.

relevant alternative to Humean constructivism. Might this suffice for the normative case for constructivism to succeed? The case for Humean constructivism along these lines strikes me as rather shaky. Consider again Great Books Theory. GBT may (in the eyes of many) yield plausible claims about what we ought and ought not do, but this advantage is far outweighed by the normative implausibility of the grounding claim. No metaethicist in their right mind would choose GBT over skepticism about morality on normative grounds. Admittedly, Humean constructivism is not quite as idiosyncratic as GBT. Still, the grounding claim is no less difficult to believe. The notion that the reason why we should, say, refrain from torturing people for fun is ultimately that we happen to *judge* it to be wrong flies squarely in the face of common sense. Just as we should not pick GBT over skepticism about morality on normative grounds, so, I submit, we should not embrace Humean constructivism in a desperate move to avoid skepticism about morality.[259] Sometimes, saving a façade is just not worth it.

The externalist maneuver

At this point we need to consider a defensive strategy that Street seems inclined to pursue. While her Humean constructivism implies the attitude-dependence and non-categoricity of our normative *reasons*, Street appears happy to concede that moral *norms* are attitude-independent and categorical, albeit devoid of intrinsic normative force. Street appears to subscribe to morality/reasons externalism (also known as moral anti-rationalism). According to this view, a moral obligation does not conceptually involve a normative reason to comply. Instead, Street takes the extent to which moral norms are normatively binding to be a contingent matter that depends on whether the agent is a 'moral agent', that is to say, someone who happens to care about what morality requires:

> [T]he right view, according to the Humean constructivist, is that moral requirements do not bind us irrespective of our particular evaluative nature. In particular, if one lacks moral concerns altogether, then morality does not bind one. But if one is a moral agent, as opposed to just an agent, then part of what that involves is taking oneself to be bound categorically (in certain cases) with respect to what one feels like doing, what one finds pleasant and attractive, and so forth.[260]

---

259 Again, similarly Tropman, 2013, p. 135.
260 Street, 2012, p. 56.

This externalist standpoint in turn allows her to combine her Humean constructivism with the view that our moral obligations are attitude-independent and categorical. At various points, Street is prepared to admit that it would be implausible to hold that moral norms are relative to people's evaluative attitudes. For example, when discussing the case of evil Caligula, she writes: "[O]f course torturing people for fun is *immoral*; but the question we're interested in is whether an ideally coherent Caligula should (full stop) be moral."[261] Street holds that moral norms are *not* relative to people's contingent attitudes, while insisting that what we have genuinely normative reason to do is a separate question. This externalist maneuver seems to allow her to counter the above-raised objection that Humean constructivism is itself normatively implausible. It allows her to say that everybody, even evil Caligula, is under a moral obligation to refrain from torturing people for fun (although he lacks reason to comply with it). Similarly, she can agree that our moral rights and duties are not grounded in our attitudes but rather attitude-independent facts. In this way, our realist intuitions about morality can be accommodated, because morality is to some extent decoupled from the Humean framework.

But there are several problems with this externalist fallback option.[262] One obvious problem is that it requires us to buy into moral externalism, which is an unattractive prospect. Many hold that morality cannot be decoupled from normative reasons in this manner.[263] Another problem is that this maneuver works only if the above-raised challenges are not specifically concerned with genuine normativity. But it seems they are. Presumably, many would want to say that everyone, irrespective of their contingent attitudes, has a genuinely *normative* reason to refrain from torturing people for fun. Likewise, deliberation about what we *normatively* ought to do (especially in moral situations) has arguably the 'feel' of an inquiry into an attitude-independent matter of fact.

Moreover, the entire architecture of the Darwinian debunking argument threatens to fall apart if morality and normative reasons are treated as two separate issues in this way. Street has been explicit that the target of the debunking argument are genuinely *normative* beliefs and that she seeks to establish that there are no genuinely *normative* attitude-independent facts: "The target of the Darwinian Dilemma [...] is *normative* realism, and so its target includes *moral* realism only if morality is understood according to a morality/reasons internalist

---

261 Street, 2009, p. 292; see also 2012, pp. 55–57; 2016, p. 327. Note that Street thinks that there is an externalist, non-normative sense of the term 'moral reason' (2008b, pp. 221–222; 2009, p. 292).

262 For a related critique of Street's externalism, refer to Morton, 2018a.

263 E.g. Huemer, 2005; Korsgaard, 1996; Nagel, 1970; Shafer-Landau, 2003; Smith, 1994.

model."[264] Therefore, if we adopt the externalist viewpoint, our non-normative moral beliefs are no longer the target of the debunking argument. Street takes it that our moral beliefs would then escape the Darwinian Dilemma. But this is confusing. For one thing, this raises questions about the empirical side of the argument. Surely, we must assume that the evolutionary forces have shaped our moral beliefs, whether we take morality to be intrinsically normative or not. But if the target of her argument are our normative beliefs (as opposed to our moral beliefs), it requires that the evolutionary forces have shaped our normative beliefs. Is Street then assuming that the evolutionary forces have shaped both our moral *and* our normative beliefs? And if so, is this a scientifically plausible theory?

For another thing, the Darwinian debunking argument is applicable to our moral beliefs, too, even if morality should not be genuinely normative. If evolutionary forces have shaped our moral beliefs as a way of bringing about fitness-enhancing behavior and if these beliefs purport to represent attitude-independent facts, it would again seem to follow that our moral beliefs are in all likelihood completely off-track. The externalist understanding of morality does not shield our moral beliefs from evolutionary debunking. And even if morality should not be genuinely normative, it is not clear why Street should find *this* kind of moral skepticism any more acceptable. As a matter of fact, most of us *do* care about morality, that is to say, most of us *are* moral agents. As Street observes, our being moral agents, although ultimately a contingent fact, is central to our identity.[265] But this means that it would be extremely disturbing if we had to conclude that our moral beliefs, which matter a lot to us, are in all likelihood massively mistaken. If she thinks that we must reject *normative* realism (realism about genuinely normative facts) if it has radically skeptical implications, she must also reject (non-normative) *moral* realism if it has radically skeptical implications.

It is difficult to see how combining Humean constructivism about reasons with an externalist and attitude-independent account of morality is a viable option for Street. On the whole, it creates more problems than it solves. Street would probably be well-advised to revert to an internalist understanding of the normativity of morality.[266] The problem that Humean constructivism is itself normatively greatly implausible persists.

---

264 Street, 2008b, p. 218.

265 Street, 2012, pp. 56–57.

266 Although this might entail an error theory, given that she rejects the Kantian version of constructivism and endorses the semantic claim that morality is categorical. One option would be to abandon the semantic claim, proposing a slight conceptual revision to avoid error theory. Anoth-

6.4 Conclusion

Again, an evolutionary debunking argument seems to backfire in unintended ways. The Darwinian Dilemma was meant to establish Humean constructivism, but upon closer inspection both interpretations of the argument really open the door to skepticism about morality. By way of conclusion, it should be acknowledged that this negative assessment of the Darwinian case for Humean constructivism should not prevent anyone from providing a non-Darwinian argument for Humean constructivism. As it turns out, Street has outlined an explicitly non-Darwinian and non-normative justification of Humean constructivism, thereby somewhat contradicting her suggestion to treat metaethical disputes as essentially normative ones. She claims that constructivism is supported by "observations about what is constitutively involved in making a normative judgment in the first place", which she explicitly characterizes as "an exercise in descriptive philosophical analysis as opposed to a substantive normative one."[267] Whether a constitutivist argument along these lines can be made to work remains to be seen. The claim that value judgments constitutively involve that all reasons are ultimately grounded in our own evaluative attitudes is, it is fair to say, a rather bold claim to make that stands in need of further validation. Street focuses primarily on demonstrating that the attitude of valuing, that is, of judging there to be a reason to perform some action, constitutively requires that one also judge that one must take what one considers the necessary means to that end.[268] While this may or may not be true, it is a far cry from showing that the attitude of valuing constitutively involves that all values are ultimately grounded in people's value judgments.[269] An improved version of such a constitutivist argument may be made to work. But until this argument has been provided, we must conclude that the case for Humean constructivism – Darwinian and non-Darwinian – is unconvincing.

---

er option would be to bite the error-theoretic bullet, which is not as unpalatable as it seems. It would not mean that our beliefs that cheating is to be condemned, etc. are *wrong*. It would merely mean that they do not qualify as 'moral' in the strict sense of the term, which might be tolerable.

267 Street, 2008a, p. 323 and 2010, p. 374, respectively.

268 Street, 2008a, pp. 227–231.

269 Similarly, Berker, 2014, pp. 240–244.

7 Morality, Wellbeing, and Evolution

7.1 Introduction

The preceding chapters have demonstrated how difficult it is to 'handle' evolutionary debunking arguments and to contain their skeptical force. The attempt to debunk deontology in order to vindicate consequentialism was shown to backfire by undermining the utilitarian project in much the same way. And the Darwinian argument for constructivism really seems to result in skepticism about morality rather than Humean constructivism. The present chapter completes this narrative by showing how the evolutionary case for skepticism about morality, compellingly made by Richard Joyce, itself collapses into skepticism about both moral and prudential normative facts. This finding will also vitiate Joyce's attempt to salvage morality as fiction.

While Street's evolutionary debunking argument focuses on the contents of our moral beliefs, Joyce's argument focuses on our moral concepts. Rather than to argue that what we believe to be morally right and wrong can be explained in evolutionary terms, he suggests that the very fact that we make moral judgments and think in moral categories in the first place is an evolutionary adaptation. Evolution being an off-track process, it means that we are not justified to believe that any moral facts exists. We should become skeptics about morality.[270]

This is the same skeptical conclusion that I suggested we should draw if we operate within a realist framework and assume, as Street does, that all our individual moral beliefs are undermined by evolutionary debunking. There are thus two different evolutionary debunking routes that lead to the same skeptical conclusion, one focusing on the contents of our moral beliefs and the other focusing on our moral concepts. In this last chapter, I demonstrate how specifically this latter debunking approach can be taken even further to undermine our prudential beliefs, too.

7.2 The evolutionary debunking of morality

In a nutshell, Joyce's evolutionary argument for skepticism about morality looks as follows:

---

270 See in particular Joyce, 2001, ch. 6; 2006, 2016a.

https://doi.org/10.1515/9783110750195-008

The Evolutionary Argument for Skepticism about Morality

P_M1: There is a plausible evolutionary explanation of why we believe in the existence of moral facts that invokes only natural facts.

P_M2: If the explanation of the belief in moral facts does not invoke any moral facts, the belief is unjustified.

P_M3: Moral facts are not reducible to natural facts.

C_M: The belief in moral facts is unjustified.

The evolutionary explanation of morality suggested by Joyce starts from the premise that evolution has selected helpful behavior, that is, behavior that benefits other individuals. He then hypothesizes that our moral sense, our faculty of making moral judgments, was selected as a means to bring about helpful behavior. Prudential reasoning is too unreliable to be entrusted with this important task. Moral norms, however, possess what Joyce calls practical clout. They exert a specific kind of normative pressure that can be analyzed as being both authoritative and inescapable. Moral norms, unlike for instance rules of etiquette, are authoritative in that they provide a "reason of genuine deliberative weight to comply."[271] And they are inescapable, or categorical, in that they apply to all agents irrespective of their contingent pro-attitudes. Belief in norms with moral clout may thus work as a bulwark against the frailty of prudential reason and is likely to have evolved as a means of achieving helpfulness. Since, as Joyce argues, moral facts are not reducible to natural facts, this purely naturalistic explanation of our belief in moral facts does not invoke any such facts. And this in turn defeats the justification of the belief in moral facts. It would be ontologically profligate to posit the existence of moral facts if positing them is not necessary to explain our belief in them.[272] Joyce's evolutionary argument purports to establish what I have called skepticism about morality. If sound, the argument shows

---

271 Joyce, 2006, p. 62.

272 A bit surprisingly, Joyce writes that his argument requires that moral facts cannot be shown to reduce to *or supervene upon* the natural facts that feature in the genealogy (see e.g 2006, p. 184; 2013b, p. 143; 2016b, 376; 2016c). But this is too concessive. According to Joyce, we should abandon our belief in moral facts if positing such facts "amount[s] to adding any extra ontological richness to the world" beyond the ontological material that is implied by the naturalistic explanation of our belief in morality (2006, p. 189). However, a moral property that merely supervenes on, while not being identical with, natural properties is certainly such an 'ontological extra'. Therefore, one cannot resist Joyce's argument by merely demonstrating that moral facts *supervene* upon natural facts. Also, the supervenience of the moral on the natural is virtually universally accepted. If mere supervenience sufficed to resist his skeptical challenge, Joyce's debunking argument would be a non-starter.

that, barring independent evidence to the contrary[273], we are not justified to believe that there are any moral facts at all. The argument yields only partial evaluative skepticism as it targets only morality. Prudential normativity is not affected by this argument.[274] Joyce's exemption of prudential normativity from his evolutionary critique is in line with his other metaethical writings, in which he has outlined the case for moral fictionalism, the view that we have prudential reasons to retain moral discourse as a fiction.[275] In what follows, I will suggest that Joyce's partial evaluative skepticism is bound to collapse into a more sweeping sort of evaluative skepticism. It is hard to resist the further conclusion that our prudential normative beliefs lack justification, too. The argument that Joyce employs to undermine our moral beliefs can plausibly be co-opted to also challenge our prudential beliefs. Just as there is a debunking explanation of why we judge our actions in moral terms, so too there is a plausible debunking explanation of why we judge our actions in prudential terms. It is therefore arguable that we should be skeptical about the existence of both moral and prudential facts.[276]

When we talk about a person's prudential good, we mean this person's 'self-interest', 'welfare', 'wellbeing', or 'advantage'. These terms are typically used interchangeably and denote the idea that a person's life can be evaluated with regard to how it is going for this person, as opposed to, say, from a moral or aesthetic perspective. I will assume that the concept of a person's prudential good (or self-interest, welfare etc.) is normative in that it involves pro tanto reasons for the agent to desire or promote it. It would be absurd for someone to understand that something is in her own interest but to not actually take any normative interest in it, that is, to not regard it as something worth desiring or pursuing. By

---

273 On the possibility of acquiring such independence evidence, see Joyce, 2006, p. 211; 2013b, p. 143; 2016c, p. 152; 2017, p. 108.

274 Joyce, 2006, pp. 227–228.

275 Joyce, 2001, 2005, 2007, 2019. His case for moral fictionalism is only provisional, though. He acknowledges that the usefulness of moral discourse is just a plausible empirical hypothesis rather than an established fact (2001, p. 228). At one point, he claims to be ambivalent between fictionalism and eliminativism (2020, p. 108).

276 Joyce does not seem to have anticipated this possible extension of his line of reasoning. An argument to the same effect has, however, been sketched by Cline (2018). But just like Kahane, Cline appears to lump together Joyce-style and Street-style debunking. Refer also to Cline's article for insightful discussions of a range of related problems with Joyce's partial evaluative skepticism.

contrast, the claim that we ought to promote the welfare of others is, while plausible, best seen as a substantive moral claim.[277]

Prudential facts are thus like moral facts in that they possess practical authority. Prudential considerations involve normative reasons to behave in a certain way. However, prudential normativity differs from morality in that it does not conceptually involve categorical force. As mentioned above, Joyce regards categoricity as a non-negotiable platitude associated with the concept of morality. For a system of norms to be recognizable as a genuinely moral one, it must centrally involve norms that apply to everybody irrespective of their contingent pro-attitudes. The same does not hold true for prudential normativity. The notion that a person's good differs from person to person is certainly not conceptually confused. On the contrary, it is quite natural to think that one's personal good is, precisely, something very personal and that people's personal goods therefore differ. Relatedly, it may be held that prudential normativity is attitude-dependent. Peter Railton, and many following him, have felt that "it capture[s] an important feature of the concept of intrinsic value to say that what is intrinsically valuable for a person must have a connection with what he would find in some degree compelling or attractive, at least if he were rational and aware."[278] I would not go so far as to regard non-categoricity and attitude-dependence as non-negotiable platitudes associated with the concept of prudential normativity. We should not rule out on conceptual grounds objective list accounts of prudential goodness, which involve categorical and attitude-independent normativity. Rather, I will make the weaker assumption that the concept of prudential goodness is at least compatible with non-categoricity and attitude-dependence.[279]

It is worth stressing that the categorical/non-categorical distinction and the attitude-independent/attitude-dependent distinction are not the same. The first distinction concerns the 'escapability' of the normativity in question. A prudential reason is categorical if everyone has this prudential reason, irrespective of their attitudes. The second distinction specifies in virtue of what the normative facts obtain, whether they are determined by our pro-attitudes or not. Although distinct, these two distinctions are related. In particular, it is often assumed that categoricity requires attitude-independence. These issues will become relevant later in our discussion.

---

277 This analysis is not undisputed (see e.g. Darwall, 2002), but it is arguably the one that comes closest to being the standard view (see e.g. Darwall, 2002, p. 4; Rodogno, 2016, p. 289).
278 Railton, 1986, p. 9.
279 The argument of this chapter does not depend on this weaker assumption. It would work just as well if we assumed that a person's prudential good involves attitude-dependent and/or non-categorical normativity as a matter of conceptual necessity.

This chapter is structured as follows: I will begin by further clarifying the nature of the suggested debunking of prudential beliefs. I then suggest a genealogical explanation of our belief in prudential facts, on which my extension of Joyce's argument rests, before engaging with four possible objections to the suggested debunking of prudential beliefs. I respond to the objection that belief in prudential facts cannot be debunked because prudential facts are attitude-dependent. I consider and dismiss the plausibility of a vindicatory evolutionary explanation of our prudential beliefs. I discuss the relevance of the potential non-categoricity of prudential normativity, and I assess the prospects of naturalizing prudential facts.

7.3 The backfiring problem: From moral beliefs to prudential beliefs

The best way of understanding what it means to extend Joyce's argument from morality to prudential normativity is to contrast it with a different way of debunking our prudential beliefs: One might argue, following Street, that evolutionary forces have had a pervasive distorting influence on the extension (or content) of both our moral and prudential beliefs and, contrary to Street, that it is a conceptual truth that both moral and prudential facts are attitude-independent. Given the distorting influence of evolutionary forces on our evaluative beliefs, these beliefs are bound to be hopelessly mistaken. It would be a huge coincidence if we happened to have evolved to track the attitude-independent truth about moral or prudential goodness. And this time we cannot, as Street suggests, just switch to an attitude-dependent account of normativity in order to avoid this radical skepticism. If we accept the semantic claim that *all* – moral as well as prudential – facts are attitude-independent, we end up with moral and prudential skepticism.

This global evaluative debunking argument has been powerfully explored by Guy Kahane[280]. At bottom, Kahane accepts the cornerstones of Street's challenge for realist theories of value and simply rejects Street's claim that one can escape this challenge by embracing an attitude-dependent account of evaluative facts. If switching to attitude-dependence is ruled out on conceptual grounds, we must accept the radical skepticism that, according to Street, attitude-independ-

---

280 Kahane, 2011. Kahane credits it with having "considerable force" (p. 117). I should note, though, that his presentation of the argument is rather explorative in nature.

ence entails. Both our moral and prudential beliefs would be hopelessly mistaken.[281]

While this argument deserves to be taken seriously, it is not the argument I will propose. The argument I will propose is an extension of Joyce's argument rather than a variation of Street's. In particular, it does not require that prudential facts are attitude-independent. This renders the argument much more powerful, given that many reject the notion that prudential goodness is attitude-independent. Defending an attitude-dependent account of prudential facts might allow one to defuse Kahane's argument, but, as we shall see, not the argument I develop below.

The focus of Joyce's debunking argument is – unlike Street's – not on the extension of our moral beliefs but on morality as such. It is our tendency to apply moral concepts and make moral judgments in the first place that Joyce takes to be amenable to an evolutionary explanation.[282] "Were it not for a certain social ancestry affecting our biology, the argument goes, we wouldn't have concepts like *obligation, virtue, property, desert,* and *fairness* at all."[283] As a consequence, we should

> cultivate agnosticism regarding all positive beliefs involving these concepts until we find some solid evidence either for or against them. Note how radical this conclusion is. It is not a matter of allowing oneself to have an open mind about, say, the wrongness of abortion or the rightness of canceling Third World debt; rather, it is a matter of maintaining an open mind about whether there exists *anything* that is morally right and wrong, of accepting the possibility that describing the world in moral terms is in the same ballpark as taking horoscopes seriously or believing that ancestral spirits move invisibly among us (as John Mackie argued is the case).[284]

I have referred to this as skepticism about morality. It is akin to moral error theory, which Joyce has defended elsewhere and which he advocates in addition to his evolutionary skepticism about morality.[285] Error theorists assert that all

---

281 Indeed, if my reasoning in Chapter 6 is correct, it would follow that we should become skeptics about prudential facts. If none of our prudential beliefs are justified, we should not believe in the existence of any such facts to begin with.

282 See e.g. Joyce, 2001, p. 146; 2006, pp. 3–4, 132, 180–181; 2013e, pp. 558–561. Kahane is somewhat insensitive to this difference, although he briefly acknowledges in a footnote that Joyce might actually be concerned with moral concepts rather than with the extension of moral beliefs (2011, p. 123 n53).

283 Joyce, 2006, p. 181.

284 Joyce, 2006, pp. 181–182.

285 Joyce, 2001, 2005. Indeed, Joyce used to think of his evolutionary skepticism about morality as a sort of moral error theory (2006, p. 223). But he has rightly observed that this skepticism

moral judgments are untrue because moral properties are never instantiated to begin with.[286] According to moral error theory, moral rights and duties have the same metaphysical status as, for instance, fairies and unicorns. Joyce's evolutionary skepticism about morality is akin to, but somewhat weaker than, moral error theory in that it states that we are not justified to believe in the existence of moral facts, while it falls short of conclusively ruling out their existence. It establishes only an epistemological conclusion, namely that the belief in moral facts is unjustified.

Now, to extend Joyce's debunking of morality from morality to prudential normativity is therefore not to argue that we should be skeptics about what our prudential good consists in, but about whether there are any prudential normative facts to begin with. To amend Joyce's formulation accordingly: Were it not for a certain social ancestry affecting our biology, the argument goes, we wouldn't have concepts like *prudential reason, self-interest* or *personal good* at all. We should therefore cultivate agnosticism regarding all positive beliefs involving these concepts until we find some solid evidence either for or against them. It is not a matter of allowing oneself to have an open mind about, say, the prudential wrongness of living a life in solitude or the prudential rightness of developing one's talents; rather, it is a matter of maintaining an open mind about whether there exists *anything* that is prudentially right and wrong, of accepting the possibility that describing the world in terms of prudential goodness is in the same ballpark as taking horoscopes seriously or believing that ancestral spirits move invisibly among us.

The argument for this position, of course, requires a plausible evolutionary story of how we may have evolved to think in terms of 'good for me' and 'bad for me'. But the belief in prudential facts is maybe even more readily amenable to an evolutionary explanation than belief in morality. We need only assume that our brute drives and desires did not work sufficiently well from an evolutionary point of view. Sometimes, acting on whatever craving just happened to be strongest led to suboptimal outcomes for the individual. It was therefore adaptive to have a notion of one's own prudential good that is distinct from the fulfilment of one's strongest desires. It was adaptive to think that one's own life can go better or worse and that this implies that certain actions are normatively called-for. Belief in prudential normative facts allowed for the necessary fine-tuning of our sometimes-detrimental desires or inclinations. Just as it is plausible to assume

does not rule out the existence of moral facts, which is why it should be distinguished from moral error theory (2013d, pp. 354–355; 2017, p. 107).

286 On some of the intricacies of characterizing moral error theory, see Joyce, 2001, pp. 6–9; Joyce and Kirchin, 2010, pp. xi-xv.

that moral considerations were a useful complement to our sometimes unreliable prudential deliberations, as Joyce suggests, so it is plausible to assume that
belief in prudential normative facts had the function of correcting maladaptive
drives and desires.[287] Based on this genealogical hypothesis, we can substitute
'prudential facts' for 'moral facts' in Joyce's argument and formulate a parallel
debunking argument of prudential beliefs:

> *The Evolutionary Argument for Skepticism about Prudential Facts*
>
> P_p1) There is a plausible evolutionary explanation of why we believe in the existence of
> prudential facts that invokes only natural facts.
>
> P_p2) If the explanation of the belief in prudential facts does not invoke any prudential
> facts, the belief is unjustified.
>
> P_p3) Prudential facts are not reducible to natural facts.
>
> C_p) The belief in prudential facts is unjustified.

P_p1, the genealogical premise, has just been laid out. The epistemological premise, P_p2, is the same as in Joyce's argument for skepticism about morality and
will not be defended here. My argument is in the first instance a conditional
one: *if* one accepts Joyce's approach, one must accept skepticism about prudential facts, too. The metaphysical premise, P_p3, is so far unargued-for and will be
considered shortly.

Needless to say, the genealogical hypothesis suggested above is, precisely, a
hypothesis, which stands in need of further empirical corroboration. Like other
debunkers and proponents of backfiring objections, I must stress the conditional
nature of the argument.[288] It rests on a plausible but unproven empirical conjecture. Unfortunately, the question concerning the potential evolutionary source of
our thinking in prudential categories has, to my knowledge, received virtually
no sustained scholarly attention.[289] It may well be that its evolutionary origin

---

287 In Chapter 2, I suggested that a similar reasoning can explain why one might think that idealizing subjectivism provides the correct account of wellbeing. Here, I am only suggesting that it
may explain why we have a notion of wellbeing at all, be it subjectivist (attitude-dependent) or
objectivist (attitude-independent).
288 See e. g. Joyce, 2001, p. 135; 2006, p. 2; 2016d, p. 9; Kahane, 2011; Mason, 2011, p. 454; Morton, 2016, p. 240; Street, 2006, pp. 112–113.
289 See, however, Machery and Mallon's discussion of evidence to the effect that normative
cognition in general rather than specifically *moral* cognition evolved (Machery and Mallon,
2010). Drawing on this evidence, they consider a backfiring objection similar to the one outlined
in this chapter (see also again Cline, 2018). Also, it is worth noting that there is evidence that
children are able to distinguish between moral and prudential rules at a fairly early age

has simply been taken for granted, given that the belief in some normative notion of self-interest fits fairly naturally into the evolutionary framework. Whereas belief in moral obligations is at least initially puzzling from an evolutionary point of view, belief in prudential dos and don'ts is rather unsurprising. In any case, while further research is necessary, I take it that the evolutionary hypothesis is plausible enough to warrant taking seriously its metaethical implications. In the remainder of this chapter, I will engage with the four already mentioned objections to this suggested debunking of prudential normativity.

The objection from attitude-dependence

I have suggested that we cannot rule out on conceptual grounds that prudential facts are attitude-dependent and/or non-categorical. Given that the attitude-dependent approach to prudential normativity is a viable option, it may appear fairly straightforward to rebut the suggested debunking of our prudential beliefs. For if prudential facts can plausibly be argued to be a function of our evaluative attitudes, how could these attitudes possibly fail to track them? Evaluative beliefs are only debunkable if they purport to represent some attitude-independent evaluative reality 'out there', or so one might reason. This would be a decisive reason to be skeptical about the viability of extending Joyce's argument from morality to prudential normativity.

Before I respond, let me briefly dwell on why this objection might appear more promising when raised against efforts to debunk prudential beliefs than when raised against Joyce's debunking of morality. Why could one not similarly allege that *moral* facts are a function of people's idealized pro-attitudes? The reason why this move is problematic is *not* that Joyce attaches great significance to the (purported) attitude-independence of morality. His focus is on the *categoricity* of moral normativity. He does not consider attitude-independence a platitude associated with the concept of morality, and the (purported) attitude-independence of morality plays no role in the hypothesized evolutionary genealogy.[290] There is, however, a more indirect link between categoricity and attitude-independence. Joyce believes that categoricity, which *is* essential to morality, cannot be captured by an approach that ties normative facts to people's

---

(Tisak and Turiel, 1984). Joyce interprets this as evidence for the innateness of our moral sense, but it can equally be seen as evidence of the innateness of our prudential sense (see Joyce, 2006, p. 135).

290 Joyce, 2013b, p. 143; 2017, p. 107.

idealized pro-attitudes.[291] If this is true, the prospects of an attitude-dependent account of morality are dim. By contrast, since it is arguable that prudential normativity, unlike morality, does not conceptually involve categoricity, an attitude-dependent account of prudential goodness cannot be ruled out on these grounds.

Let us consider, then, whether the potential attitude-dependence of prudential facts undermines the suggested debunking explanation. It is assumed by many that debunking arguments of the sort put forth by Street, Greene and Singer are toothless against judgments about attitude-dependent values.[292] If this is true, it is tempting to reject attempts to debunk prudential beliefs on the grounds that prudential facts are attitude-dependent. But this objection fails to attend to the above-discussed difference between Kahane's argument and the one I am suggesting. The objection would have force if I were challenging our ability to track what the prudential facts consist in, assuming that such facts exist. That is, it would have force against Kahane's argument, which is indeed premised on the attitude-independence of prudential facts. One might then reckon that our evaluative attitudes cannot be that far off the mark given that the prudential facts are actually *not* attitude-independent but a function of our attitudes. But the argument I am making is not best understood as being about our ability to 'track' the prudential truth. It is analogous to Joyce's argument, and Joyce's worry is not that we might be mistaken about what our moral duties consist in. Rather, he contends that morality as such may be an illusion. Analogously, I am not questioning our ability to correctly track what the prudential facts consist in. Rather, I am alleging that we are not justified to believe in the existence of prudential facts to begin with. An objection to the effect that we are probably good at 'tracking' these facts, taking their existence for granted, is therefore a non-starter. It may be true that *if* we assume that there are prudential facts and that they depend on our attitudes, the prospects of correctly identifying them might not be too bleak. For these prudential facts would be constructed by our attitudes. However, what is not constructed by our attitudes is the fact that there are prudential facts that depend on our attitudes in the first place, that is, that certain facts about our attitudes instantiate prudential normative facts at all. It is this fact that is the target of the suggested debunking argument, and whether *this* fact obtains is attitude-independent. Adopting an attitude-de-

291 Although this might not apply to divine-command theory, which ties normative facts to God's judgments (Joyce, 2013b, p. 144 n4).
292 Most prominently, of course, by Street. But see also Gill and Nichols, 2008; Kahane, 2011, p. 112; 2014a, p. 339; Levy, 2006; Nichols, 2014, pp. 748–749; Timmons, 2008.

pendent framework of prudential normativity is of no avail if there are no prudential facts to be tracked in the first place.

Note that this means that the objection would also fail if raised against Joyce's debunking of morality. Let us assume, for the sake of argument, that an attitude-dependent approach that ties reasons to people's idealized pro-attitudes could yield categorical reasons (contrary to what Joyce is assuming). That is, an attitude-dependent theory of morality could not be ruled out on the grounds that it fails to account for the categorical normativity that is essential to morality. Could a champion of such a theory object to Joyce's debunking of morality by insisting that we cannot be that bad at tracking our moral reasons given that the latter are more or less closely tied to our pro-attitudes? It does not seem so, for Joyce's argument does not challenge our ability to correctly identify our moral reasons but rather the assumption that there are any moral facts to being with. It purports to establish skepticism about whether moral properties are instantiated at all, no matter whether they are grounded in people's pro-attitudes or not. As Joyce observes, his "skeptical attack is leveled at moral facts *tout court* – subjective as much as objective."[293]

The objection from the analogy with sensory perception

The above discussion also helps us see why another objection fails. One might be tempted to dismiss the suggested debunking explanation of prudential beliefs on the grounds that the evolutionary explanation actually vindicates, rather than undermines, our prudential normative beliefs. The proposed evolutionary explanation of our tendency to think in prudential categories would then be analogous to evolutionary explanations of the emergence of our sensory organs, which are vindicatory rather than debunking explanations. The reason why the correct perception of one's prudential good may be thought to be analogous to sensory perception is that the correct perception of one's prudential good is in one's own interest and therefore presumably conducive to reproduction. It may appear obvious that a properly working capability to detect our prudential reasons is, just like properly working sensory organs, useful from an evolutionary point of view.

One reason why this objection fails is that it rests on an equivocation. It tacitly conflates the normative notion of a person's prudential good with the em-

---

293 Joyce, 2013a, p. 467; see also 2013b, p. 143; 2017, p. 107. Joyce uses the terms 'subjective' and 'objective' to mean 'attitude-dependent' and 'attitude-independent', respectively.

pirical concept of what is good from an evolutionary point of view, that is, with what enhances our reproductive fitness. But these are of course two different concepts. And once this difference is appreciated, the intuitive plausibility of the analogy with sensory perception vanishes. There is no apparent reason why it should be beneficial from an evolutionary point of view to be right about what one's actual prudential good consists in.[294] More importantly, however, the objection from the analogy with sensory perception fails for the same reason as the previous objection, the one from attitude-dependence. The suggested debunking argument is not meant to cast doubt on our ability to *correctly identify* our prudential reasons for action, that is, it is not meant to entail skepticism about what our reasons for action *consist in*. Rather, the argument is concerned with prudential normativity as such, that is, with our tendency to imbue courses of action with a certain prudential normative valence. Instead of merely desiring certain courses of action, we feel a normative pull towards them, we feel that there is something prudentially speaking in favor of performing them. It is the belief in this kind of normativity that is vulnerable to a debunking explanation. The analogy with our sensory organs is therefore misleading. The ability to make correct judgments about whether there is such a thing as prudential normativity in the first place is *not* relevantly similar to the ability to correctly detect mid-sized physical objects in our environment. Thinking in terms of prudential 'oughts' is adaptive even if no such normative properties are ever instantiated. This contrasts sharply with sensory perception. An evolutionary account of why we believe in the existence of prudential facts does therefore not amount to a vindication of these beliefs. On the contrary.

The objection from non-categoricity

A third objection concerns the potential non-categoricity of prudential normativity. The inescapability of moral norms plays an important role in the genealogical

---

294 Third-factor accounts might offer a way around this problem. But to pursue a third-factor approach would be to *abandon* the perception analogy. The perception analogy states that we have evolved to reliably track facts about prudential goodness *because* the capacity to track these facts promotes reproductive success. A third-factor account, by contrast, while agreeing that evolutionary forces have pushed us towards the evaluative truth, would not posit this 'because' relation. Instead, it would posit some third factor that guarantees a correlation between what is prudentially good and the evaluative beliefs that enhance reproductive fitness (see Copp's distinction between the tracking account and the tracking thesis (2008)). As noted in the introduction, the plausibility of such third-factor accounts is disputed.

story sketched by Joyce. The evolutionary benefit that morality is supposed to have bestowed on our ancestors is closely tied to the inescapability of its normative force. If, as I have suggested, prudential normativity may well lack this inescapability, it is doubtful whether prudential beliefs can have played a similar motivational role. This objection thus targets the genealogical premise of the argument.

To see whether these doubts are justified, let us look closer at the rationale behind Joyce's suggested genealogy of morality:

> My thinking on this matter is dominated by the natural assumption that an individual sincerely judging some available action in a morally positive light increases the probability that the individual will perform that action [...]. If reproductive fitness will be served by performance or omission of a certain action, then it will be served by any psychological mechanism that ensures or probabilifies this performance or omission [...]. Thus self-directed moral judgment may enhance reproductive fitness so long as it is attached to the appropriate actions. We have already seen that the 'appropriate actions' – that is, the fitness enhancing actions – will in many circumstances include helpful and cooperative behaviors. Therefore it may serve an individual's fitness to judge certain prosocial behaviors – *her own* prosocial behaviors – in moral terms.[295]

Why must the authority of moral norms be inescapable for morality to serve this function? Joyce's answer is that the inescapability of moral imperatives makes moral behavior more steady and reliable. Prudential reason is (at least sometimes) just too frail and weak-willed to be entrusted with this task. The inescapability of morality works as a motivational bulwark against this frailty of prudential reason. We are more likely to perform the called-for action if we regard a certain outcome as desir*able* rather than merely as desir*ed*, if we believe that we *must* perform the action, even if we do not like it. Our moral conscience works as a filter that "eliminates certain practical possibilities from the space of deliberative reasoning in a way that thinking 'I just don't like X' does not."[296] Joyce expressly contrasts moral reasoning with prudential reasoning. He takes belief in moral facts to be more likely to produce the adaptive behavior precisely in virtue of the inescapability that prudential norms arguably lack.[297]

---

295 Joyce, 2006, pp. 109. This is only one of the two ways in which, according to Joyce, having a moral conscience enhances one's reproductive fitness. I omit the other one as it has to do with the communicative function of morality, which is not applicable to prudential normativity (Joyce, 2006, pp. 118–123).
296 Joyce, 2006, p. 111.
297 Joyce, 2006, pp. 110–111; see also 2001, pp. 139–140; Ruse, 1986, pp. 252–253.

I do not want to challenge the assumption that the inescapability of morality contributes to morality's motivational function and that morality has emerged for the reasons suggested by Joyce. Rather, I wish to observe that all this does not prevent prudential beliefs from having a comparable motivational effect, too. Even if our prudential reasons for action are in some way or another linked to our pro-attitudes and non-categorical, awareness of these reasons may motivate us to perform actions that we would not otherwise have performed. *If* some prudential reason for action obtains (or is thought to obtain) – which may well be a contingent attitude-dependent matter – its normative authority is likely to influence the behavior of the person who takes notice of this prudential consideration for action. Note also that many of the features of morality highlighted by Joyce are characteristic of prudential normativity in much the same way, even if prudential normativity should be attitude-dependent and non-categorical. Joyce overlooks these similarities as he conflates prudential normativity with simple desiring, which are two different things. Joyce stresses that morality is about the desir*able* rather than the desired, and that we *must* do our moral duty, whether we like it or not.[298] But this is also true of prudential normativity. What we intrinsically have reason to do for our own sake is likewise not simply what we desire to do but what is prudentially desirable. To be sure, the prudentially desirable, unlike the morally desirable, may be linked to our desires, and its normative force may be non-categorical. But this does not make the prudentially good any less normative, any less desir*able*. By the same token, we *must* do what we prudentially ought to do. An 'ought' is not normatively optional just because it is a prudential rather than a moral 'ought'. Even if the validity of the prudential norm is contingent upon the agent's pro-attitudes and non-categorical, this does not mean that it is up to her whether she complies with it. The fact that an agent's prudential reason to perform some action may somehow be linked to her pro-attitudes – say, because it is what she would desire after ideal deliberation – does not imply that she is not prudentially obliged to perform this action. She cannot shrug off this prudential obligation on the grounds that she *actually* – that is, prior to ideal deliberation – does not desire to perform this action. Therefore, just like moral considerations, prudential considerations can work as a filter that 'eliminates certain practical possibilities from the space of deliberative reasoning in a way that thinking 'I just don't like X' does not'.

---

298 Joyce, 2006, p. 111.

Put more succinctly, the objection from non-categoricity fails because it ignores that belief in non-categorical reasons can probabilify fitness-enhancing behavior, too.

The objection from naturalism

The last objection concerns the metaphysical premise of the argument, P_P3. The idea underlying Joyce's debunking argument is that the evolutionary story allows us to explain people's belief in moral facts without invoking the existence of such facts. But this requires that moral facts are not reducible to natural facts, which might feature in the naturalistic genealogy. Accordingly, if we wish to extend Joyce's evolutionary debunking argument from morality to prudential normativity, it must be shown that prudential facts cannot be naturalized either. It is at this point that one might think that the potential attitude-dependence of prudential facts is relevant after all, as this seems to render prudential facts readily amenable to naturalistic reduction. So if prudential facts are attitude-dependent and do not involve categorical reasons, the attempted extension of Joyce's debunking argument from morality to prudential normativity might collapse.

While I cannot here hope to provide a conclusive discussion of the possibility of naturalizing prudential facts, I wish to at least provide some reasons to be skeptical about the prospects of this project. In particular, I will explain why Joyce's own reasoning about this question somewhat obscures the difficulty of the challenge naturalists are facing.

Joyce rejects naturalistic accounts of morality on the grounds that the most promising such accounts fail to capture the inescapability of moral normativity. Recall, inescapability – or categoricity – is one of the two constituents of what Joyce calls 'moral clout', which he considers essential to morality. The other constituent is practical authority, that is, the property of being reason-providing, of involving a practical consideration of genuine deliberative force. Joyce argues that naturalistic approaches may well capture this latter property, but they fail to do justice to the inescapability of moral reasons. Joyce takes it that the most promising approach to naturalizing moral or prudential reasons is by tying them to our idealized pro-attitudes, that is, by tying them to some such natural property as "being-such-that-you-would-want-to-do-it-if-you-were-to-reason-correctly"[299]. And he is happy to grant that this property has practical authority, that is to say, that it "represent[s] a genuine deliberative consideration" or that

---

299 Joyce, 2006, p. 196.

it "carr[ies] deliberative weight."[300] But he maintains that this account does not yield inescapable reasons:

> The problem, however, and my main ground for doubting the project, is that in order to naturalize moral clout we cannot be content just to find a property that has practical authority – arguably we have located such a property in *being-such-that-you-would-want-to-do-it-if-you-were-to-reason-correctly*. We must also satisfy *inescapability*; we need a property that has this authority over people *irrespective of their interests*. But it is doubtful that any naturalizable account can deliver this.[301]

The reason why he thinks that attitude-dependent accounts of normativity cannot capture the inescapability of morality is that there is nothing that *everybody*, no matter what pro-attitudes they happen to start from, would want to do if they were to reason correctly. Given the heterogeneity of people's contingent pro-attitudes, this idealized reasoning process is unlikely to yield categorical reasons.[302] Now, if prudential normativity does not conceptually imply categorical normativity, this objection cannot be levelled against similar attempts to naturalize prudential normativity. In light of this, the prospects of naturalizing prudential normativity do not appear too bleak.

However, when assessing the prospects of a naturalistic account of prudential normativity, it is critical to be attentive to exactly what naturalizing prudential normativity actually involves. It does not suffice – as Joyce's formulations might suggest – to provide a naturalistic account of what *are* or *provides* or *grounds* our prudential reasons. Showing that our prudential reasons are determined by what we would desire to do after ideal deliberation does not yet necessarily amount to a naturalistic reduction of prudential normativity, even if the property of being such that we would desire to do it after ideal deliberation is a natural property. It does not suffice to show that some natural property 'represents' a genuine deliberative consideration or 'carries' normative weight or 'has' practical authority. Rather, what has to be naturalized is the property, possessed by this natural property, of providing a reason for action or of carrying genuine deliberative force. What has to be naturalized is the phenomenon of practical authority itself, that is, the 'to-be-persuedness' and 'not-to-be-doneness' that is characteristic of the normative.[303] One has to naturalize *normativity* rather than just the facts that are normatively significant by being the things that

---

300 Joyce, 2006, p. 195.
301 Joyce, 2006, p. 196.
302 Joyce, 2006, p. 194–199; see also 2001, 2011.
303 These are Mackie's terms (1977, p. 40).

are or ground or provide reasons for action. I am here essentially paraphrasing Derek Parfit, who has observed that

> [w]henever some natural fact gives us a reason, there is also the normative fact that this natural fact gives us this reason. It is easy to overlook such normative facts. This mistake is especially likely if, rather than saying that certain natural facts give us reasons, we say that these facts are reasons. These are merely different ways of saying the same things. But if we say that natural facts of certain kinds are reasons to act in certain ways, we may be led to assume that, to defend the view that there are normative reasons, it is enough to defend the claim that there are natural facts of these kinds. That is not so. We must also defend the claim that these natural facts each have the normative property of being a reason. And this second claim, property, and fact might all be irreducibly normative.[304]

Of course, bringing out in this way what normativity is does not yet necessarily disprove naturalism. But it gives us an idea of the difficulty of the task the naturalist is facing. Indeed, in light of the above, it is tempting to side with those who have considered it evident that normativity *just cannot* be a natural thing. Huemer calls it the argument from radical dissimilarity:

> [F]rom our grasp of evaluative concepts, we can simply see the falsity of reductionist theories. On the face of it, for example, *wrongness* seems to be a completely different *kind* of property from, say, *weighing 5 pounds*. In brief:
> 1. Value properties are radically different from natural properties.
> 2. If two things are radically different, then one is not reducible to the other.
> 3. So value properties are not reducible to natural properties.[305]

Similarly, Derek Parfit has argued:

> Many kinds of thing, event, or fact are [...] undeniably in different categories. Rivers could not be sonnets, experiences could not be stones, and justice could not be – as some Pythagoreans were said to have believed – the number 4. [...] It is similarly true, I believe, that when we have decisive reasons to act in some way, or we should or ought to act in this way, this fact could not be the same as, or consist in, some natural fact, such as some psychological or causal fact.[306]

Of course, these brief remarks do not settle the matter. Whether normativity can be naturalized is still very much an open question, and I do not purport to have

---

304 Parfit, 2011b, p. 280; see also FitzPatrick, 2008, 2011, 2014; McNaughton and Rawling, 2003, pp. 30–31; Olson, 2009; Parfit, 1993.
305 Huemer, 2005, p. 94.
306 Parfit, 2011b, pp. 324–325

provided anything resembling a conclusive answer.[307] But the above considerations should make clear that naturalizing prudential normativity represents a formidable philosophical challenge, even if prudential normativity may be attitude-dependent and non-categorical. For even if one would not have to show that some natural property has practical authority irrespective of people's contingent interests, one would still have to show that practical authority itself is a natural thing. And whether this can be accomplished is, to say the least, doubtful.

7.4 Conclusion

There is good reason to think that the evolutionary debunking of morality cannot be prevented from spilling over to prudential normativity. This finding backfires by undermining Joyce's (tentative) case for retaining morality as a fiction. Fictionalism is the idea that we have prudential reasons to maintain moral discourse as a useful fiction. Even when we are no longer justified to believe in moral facts, it can be advisable to *pretend* to believe in moral facts. Engaging in acts of make-believe to uphold moral discourse as a fiction can nudge us towards actions that benefit us. The case for moral fictionalism is thus premised on the existence prudential reasons. There are prudential 'oughts' that speak in favor of continuing to use and think in terms of moral 'oughts'. But if the above argument is sound, we are not justified to believe in the existence of prudential 'oughts'. It no longer makes no sense to argue for retaining morality as a fiction on the grounds that it is 'good for us' or 'beneficial', because these are normative predicates that we are no longer justified to believe in.

Could we retreat one step further and adopt fictionalism about prudential normativity? Just as Joyce insists that philosophical doubts about the reality of morality do not necessarily warrant abolishing morality as an institution, one might question whether doubts about the reality of prudential normativity really requires abandoning thinking in terms of prudential 'oughts'. Unfortunately, efforts to salvage prudential normativity as a fiction are rather obviously bound to fail, as it is unclear on what grounds we should adopt fictionalism about prudential normativity. Joyce's moral fictionalism rests on the assumption that we have got prudential reasons to accept morality as a fiction. But we can hardly appeal to such prudential reasons in an attempt to vindicate fictionalism about prudential normativity. We would have to appeal to *independent* reasons to adopt pru-

---

307 See e.g. Copp, 2012 for a subtle critique of Parfit's arguments against naturalism.

dential discourse as a fiction, and it is unclear what these reasons might be. The prospects of grounding prudential fictionalism on aesthetic or epistemic reasons are dim

If anything, we might end up as prudential fictionalists for the simple reason that we just cannot help but think in terms of prudential 'oughts'. Even if we are aware of philosophical considerations that challenge the reality of prudential normativity, we might be psychologically unable to stop thinking in prudential terms. Rather than to actively decide to maintain prudential discourse as a useful fiction because this decision is supported by reason, it is conceivable that we end up carrying on with prudential discourse because it is psychologically near impossible not to think in prudential categories. We might then also maintain morality as a fiction based on (fictitious) prudential grounds. But whether all this would be 'good for us' is a moot question.

8 Conclusion

Philosophy's renewed interest in genealogical arguments has been overdue. The assumption, long implicit or explicit in much analytic philosophy, that we need not be concerned with how philosophical beliefs and theories have originated reflects a misconception about the distinctness of 'genesis' and 'validity'. Arguably, this misconception has been a considerable hindrance to philosophical progress. The case for taking into account genealogical information is particularly compelling for moral philosophy. It has become increasingly difficult to justify doing moral philosophy without paying attention to the origins of moral cognition and those of particular moral intuitions and convictions. At the same time, empirically informed ethics is very much in its infancy, and how debunking arguments should be constructed and where they lead us is still poorly understood. This book has sought to contribute to a better understanding of empirically informed ethics and debunking arguments in particular. It has revealed some of the pitfalls of drawing on genealogical information to construct debunking arguments, and it has outlined how the evolutionary debunking project can be taken even further.

One general lesson for future would-be debunkers concerns the argumentation-theoretical status of debunking arguments. While a strict division between 'genesis' and 'validity' is misguided, there is also some truth in the widely shared idea that genealogical reasoning is objectionable. We have seen that debunking arguments that rely on higher-order defeat, although not fallacies, should not be permitted in philosophical debate. Genealogical arguments should be welcomed again in philosophy, but only genealogical arguments of a certain type. Another result is that the usefulness of experimental investigations into the factors that trigger our moral responses for debunking projects is still very much in the air. Would-be debunkers are well advised to either pursue other debunking approaches, or to first elucidate the point of relying on experimental findings to construct arguments from moral irrelevance. The most important takeaway concerns the difficulty of tailoring debunking arguments to one's dialectical ambitions. The chief problem with debunking arguments is that they tend to collapse into more skeptical arguments than intended by its authors. Indeed, it is likely that the evolutionary debunking project forces us to accept skepticism about both morality and prudential facts.

I want to close by suggesting that the argument might in fact be extended even further. The target of the argument outlined in the last chapter was belief in prudential normativity. It does not challenge other normative realms, such as epistemic or aesthetic normativity. But it is only natural to wonder whether

https://doi.org/10.1515/9783110750195-009

all normative beliefs can eventually be debunked in this way. Given that thinking in normative categories has an impact on people's behavior, it is not far-fetched to surmise that our faculty of thinking in terms of 'oughts' of whatever kind is an adaptive but deceptive invention of evolution.[308] The appearance that certain responses are normatively required might be but a figment of our minds that served the function of pushing us towards fitness-enhancing behavior. Whether such a global normative debunking argument may succeed depends inter alia on whether these other normative realms can be naturalized and on the plausibility of the genealogical hypothesis. Also, attempts to debunk epistemic normativity are complicated by the fact that they threaten to be self-defeating. An argument that yields the conclusion that we are not epistemically justified to believe in facts about epistemic justification has certainly an air of contradiction about it.[309] I will not pursue these difficult questions here, but I wish to mention them as a plea for further study.

---

308 See again Machery and Mallon, 2010. See Streumer, 2017 for the similar but even stronger claim that we should become error theorists about all normative judgments. And refer to Cline, 2018 for an instructive discussion of some issues related to global normative skepticism.
309 Similarly Kahane, 2012, p. 117.

9 References

Althusser, L. (1971). Ideology and Ideological State Apparatuses. In L. Althusser (Ed.), *"Lenin and Philosophy" and Other Essays* (pp. 121–176). New York: Monthly Review Press.

Andes, P. (2019). Sidgwick's Dualism of Practical Reason, Evolutionary Debunking, and Moral Psychology. *Utilitas, 31*(4), 361–377.

Atran, S. (2002). *In Gods We Trust: The Evolutionary Landscape of Religion.* Oxford/New York: Oxford University Press.

Ballantyne, N. (2015). Debunking Biased Thinkers (Including Ourselves). *Journal of the American Philosophical Association, 1*(1), 141–162.

Barclay, P. (2006). Reputational benefits for altruistic punishment. *Evolution and Human Behavior, 27*(5), 325–344.

Barkhausen, M. (2016). Reductionist Moral Realism and the Contingency of Moral Evolution. *Ethics, 126*(3), 662–689.

Barney, R. (2011). Callicles and Thrasymachus. In E. N. Zalta (Ed.), *Stanford Encyclopedia of Philosophy*. Retrieved from <https://plato.stanford.edu/entries/callicles-thrasymachus/>

Barrett, J. L. (2000). Exploring the natural foundations of religion. *TRENDS in Cognitive Sciences, 4*(1), 29–34.

Barrett, J. L. (2004). *Why Would Anyone Believe in God?* Walnut Creek, CA: AltaMira Press.

Barrett, J. L. (2007). Is the spell really broken? Bio-psychological explanations of religion and theistic belief. *Theology and Science, 5*(1), 57–72.

Behrends, J. (2013). Meta-Normative Realism, Evolution, and Our Reasons to Survive. *Pacific Philosophical Quarterly, 94*(4), 486–502.

Benacceraf, P. (1973). Mathematical Truth. *The Journal of Philosophy, 70*(19), 661–679.

Berker, S. (2009). The Normative Insignificance of Neuroscience. *Philosophy and Public Affairs, 37*(4), 293–329.

Berker, S. (2014). Does Evolutionary Psychology Show That Normativity Is Mind-Dependent? In J. D'Arms and D. Jacobson (Eds.), *Moral Psychology and Human Agency* (pp. 215–252). Oxford/New York: Oxford University Press.

Biro, J., and Siegel, H. (1992). Normativity, Argumentation and an Epistemic Theory of Fallacies. In F. H. van Eemeren, R. Grootendorst, J. A. Blair, and C. A. Willard (Eds.), *Argumentation Illuminated* (pp. 85–103). Amsterdam: Sic Sat.

Biro, J., and Siegel, H. (2006). Pragma-Dialectic Versus Epistemic Theories of Arguing and Argumentation. In P. Houtlosser and A. van Rees (Eds.), *Considering Pragma-Dialectics* (pp. 1–10). New York/London: Routledge.

Bogardus, T. (2016). Only All Naturalists Should Worry About Only One Evolutionary Debunking Argument. *Ethics, 126*(3), 636–661.

Boonin, D. (2008). *The Problem of Punishment.* Cambridge: Cambridge University Press.

Bowles, S., and Gintis, H. (2004). The Evolution of Strong Reciprocity: Cooperation in Heterogenous Populations. *Theoretical Population Biology, 65*(1), 17–28.

Boyd, R., et al. (2003). The evolution of altruistic punishment. *Proceedings of the National Academy of Sciences, 100*(6), 3531–3535.

Boyer, P. (2001). *Religion Explained: The Evolutionary Origins of Religious Thought.* New York: Basic Books.

Braddock, M. C. (2017). Debunking arguments from sensitivity. *International Journal for the Study of Skepticism, 7*(2), 1–23.

https://doi.org/10.1515/9783110750195-010

Bramble, B. (2017). Evolutionary Debunking Arguments and our Shared Hatred of Pain. *Journal of Ethics and Social Philosophy, 12*(1), 94–101.

Brandt, R. (1979). *A Theory of the Good and the Right.* Oxford: Oxford University Press.

Brennan, J., and Jaworski, P. M. (2015). Markets Without Symbolic Limits. *Ethics, 125*(4), 1053–1077.

Brennan, J., and Jaworski, P. M. (2016). *Markets Without Limits: Moral Virtues and Commercial Interests.* New York/London: Routledge.

Brosnan, K. (2011). Do the evolutionary origins of our moral beliefs undermine moral knowledge? *Biology & Philosophy, 26*(1), 51–64.

Bruers, S., and Braeckman, J. (2014). A Review and Systematization of the Trolley Problem. *Philosophia, 42*(2), 251–269.

Bruni, T., et al. (2014). The Science of Morality and its Normative Implications. *Neuroethics, 7*(2), 159–172.

Buss, D. M. (2014). *Evolutionary Psychology: The New Science of the Mind.* London/New York: Routledge.

Campbell, R., and Kumar, V. (2012). Moral Reasoning on the Ground. *Ethics, 122*(2), 273–312.

Christensen, D. (2010). Higher-Order Evidence. *Philosophy and Phenomenological Research, 81*(1), 185–215.

Clarke-Doane, J. (2015). Justification and Explanation in Mathematics and Morality. In R. Shafer-Landau (Ed.), *Oxford Studies in Metaethics: Volume 10* (pp. 80–103). Oxford: Oxford University Press.

Clarke-Doane, J. (2016). Debunking and Dispensability. In U. D. Leibowitz and N. Sinclair (Eds.), *Explanations in Ethics and Mathematics: Debunking and Dispensability* (pp. 23–36). Oxford: Oxford University Press.

Clarke-Doane, J. (2020). *Mathematics and Morality.* Oxford: Oxford University Press.

Clarke-Doane, J., and Baras, D. (2021). Modal Security. *Philosophy and Phenomenological Research, 102*(1), 162–183.

Cline, B. (2018). The tale of the moderate normative skeptic. *Philosophical Studies, 175*(1), 141–161.

Cohen, G. A. (2000). *If You're an Egalitarian, How Come You're So Rich?* Cambridge, MA: Harvard University Press.

Coleman, E. (1995). There is no Fallacy of Arguing from Authority. *Informal Logic, 17*(3), 365–383.

Conway, P., et al. (2018). Sacrificial utilitarian judgments do reflect concern for the greater good: Clarification via process dissociation and the judgments of philosophers. *Cognition, 179*, 241–265.

Copp, D. (2008). Darwinian Skepticism About Moral Realism. *Philosophical Issues, 18*(1), 186–206.

Copp, D. (2012). Normativity and reasons: five arguments from Parfit against normative naturalism. In S. Nuccetelli and G. Seay (Eds.), *Ethical Naturalism: Current Debates* (pp. 24–57). Cambridge: Cambridge University Press.

Copp, D. (2019). How to avoid begging the question against evolutionary debunking arguments. *Ratio, 32*(4), 231–245.

Cowie, C. (2020). Contemporary Work on Debunking Arguments in Morality and Mathematics. In C. Cowie and R. Rowland (Eds.), *Companions in Guilt Arguments in Metaethics* (pp. 135–149). Abingdon: Routledge.

Crockett, M. J. (2013). Model of morality. *TRENDS in Cognitive Sciences, 17*(8), 363–366.

Cushman, F. (2013). Action, Outcome, and Value: A Dual-System Framework for Morality. *Personality and Social Psychology Review, 17*(3), 273–292.

Cushman, F., et al. (2006). The Role of Conscious Reasoning and Intuition in Moral Judgment: Testing Three Principles of Harm. *Psychological Science, 17*(12), 1082–1089.

Cushman, F., et al. (2010). Multi-system Moral Psychology. In J. M. Doris and the Moral Psychology Research Group (Eds.), *The Moral Psychology Handbook* (pp. 47–71). Oxford/New York: Oxford University Press.

Dale, M. T. (2020). Neurons and Normativity: A Critique of Greene's Notion of Unfamiliarity. *Philosophical Psychology, 33*(8), 1072–1095.

Darwall, S. (2002). *Welfare and Rational Care*. Princeton, NJ: Princeton University Press.

Das, R. (2016). Evolutionary Debunking of Morality: Epistemological or Metaphysical? *Philosophical Studies, 173*(2), 417–435.

Dawkins, R. (1976). *The Selfish Gene*. Oxford: Oxford University Press.

Dawkins, R. (2007). *The God Delusion*. London: Black Swan.

de Lazari-Radek, K., and Singer, P. (2012). The Objectivity of Ethics and the Unity of Practical Reason. *Ethics, 123*(1), 9–31.

de Lazari-Radek, K., and Singer, P. (2014). *The Point of View of the Universe: Sidgwick and Contemporary Ethics*. Oxford: Oxford University Press.

Dean, R. (2010). Does Neuroscience Undermine Deontological Theory? *Neuroethics, 3*(1), 43–60.

Dennett, D. (2007). *Breaking the Spell: Religion as a Natural Phenomenon*. London: Penguin Books.

DePaul, M. (2006). Intutions in Moral Inquiry. In D. Copp (Ed.), *The Oxford Handbook of Ethical Theory* (pp. 595–623). New York: Oxford University Press.

Dutton, D. G., and Aron, A. P. (1974). Some evidence for heightened sexual attraction under conditions of high anxiety. *Journal of Personality and Social Psychology, 30*(4), 510–517.

Dworkin, R. (1996). Objectivity and Truth: You'd Better Believe It. *Philosophy and Public Affairs, 25*(2), 87–139.

Dyke, M. M. (2020). Bad bootstrapping: the problem with third-factor replies to the Darwinian Dilemma for moral realism. *Philosophical Studies, 177*(8), 2115–2128.

Eagleton, T. (1991). *Ideology: An Introduction*. London: Verso.

Enoch, D. (2007). An Outline for an Argument for Robust Metanormative Realism. In R. Shafer-Landau (Ed.), *Oxford Studies in Metaethics: Volume 2* (pp. 21–50). Oxford/New York: Oxford University Press.

Enoch, D. (2010). The epistemological challenge to metanormative realism: how best to understand it, and how to cope with it. *Philosophical Studies, 148*(3), 413–438.

Enoch, D. (2014). Why I am an Objectivist about Ethics (And Why You Are, Too). In R. Shafer-Landau (Ed.), *The Ethical Life: Fundamental Readings in Ethics and Moral Problems (3rd edition)* (pp. 192–205). New York: Oxford University Presss.

Ernst, Z. (2007). The Liberationists' Attack on Moral Intuitions. *American Philosophical Quarterly, 44*(2), 129–142.

Estlund, D. (2014). Utopophobia. *Philosophy and Public Affairs, 42*(2), 113–134.

Evans, J. S. B. T. (2008). Dual-Processing Accounts of Reasoning, Judgment, and Social Cognition. *Annual Review of Psychology, 59*(1), 255.

Evans, J. S. B. T. (2011). Dual-process theories of reasoning: Contemporary issues and developmental applications. *Developmental Review, 31*(2–3), 86–102.

Feldman, R. (2005). Respecting the Evidence. *Philosophical Perspectives, 19*(1), 95–119.

Feldman, R. (2006). Epistemological puzzles about disagreement. In S. Hetherington (Ed.), *Epistemological Futures* (pp. 216–236). Oxford: Oxford University Press.

Field, H. (1989). *Realism, Mathematics, and Modality.* Oxford: Blackwell.

FitzPatrick, W. J. (2008). Robust Ethical Realism, Non-Naturalism, and Normativity. In R. Shafer-Landau (Ed.), *Oxford Studies in Metaethics: Volume 3* (pp. 159–205). Oxford: Oxford University Press.

FitzPatrick, W. J. (2011). Ethical Non-Naturalism and Normative Properties. In M. Brady (Ed.), *New Waves in Metaethics* (pp. 7–35). Basingstoke: Palgrave Macmillan.

FitzPatrick, W. J. (2014). Skepticism about Naturalizing Normativity: In Defense of Ethical Nonnaturalism. *Res Philosophica, 91*(4), 559–588.

FitzPatrick, W. J. (2015). Debunking evolutionary debunking of ethical realism. *Philosophical Studies, 172*(4), 883–904.

FitzPatrick, W. J. (2018). Cognitive Science and Moral Philosophy: Challenging Scientific Overreach. In J. d. Ridder, R. Peels, and R. v. Woudenberg (Eds.), *Scientism: Prospects and Problems* (pp. 233–257). New York: Oxford University Press.

Foot, P. (1967). The Problem of Abortion and the Doctrine of Double Effect. *Oxford Review, 5,* 5–15.

Freud, S. (1961). *The Future of an Illusion.* New York: W. W. Norton.

Gazzaniga, M. S., and LeDoux, J. E. (1978). *The Integrated Mind.* New York: Plenum.

Gill, M. B., and Nichols, S. (2008). Sentimentalist Pluralism: Moral Psychology and Philosophical Ethics. *Philosophical Issues, 18*(1), 143–163.

Gino, F., et al. (2010). Nameless + harmless = blameless: When seemingly irrelevant factors influence judgment of (un)ethical behavior. *Organizational Behavior and Human Decision Processes, 111*(2), 93–101.

Gintis, H., et al. (2001). Costly Signalling and Cooperation. *Journal of Theoretical Biology, 213*(1), 103–119.

Goldman, A. I. (1986). *Epistemology and Cognition.* Cambridge, MA/London: Harvard University Press.

Goldman, A. I. (1999). *Knowledge in a Social World.* Oxford/New York: Oxford University Press.

Graber, A. (2012). Medusa's Gaze Reflected: A Darwinian Dilemma for Anti-Realist Theories of Value. *Ethical Theory and Moral Practice, 15*(5), 589–601.

Greene, J. (2005a). Cognitive Neuroscience and the Structure of the Moral Mind. In P. Carruthers, S. Laurence, and S. Stich (Eds.), *The Innate Mind: Structure and Contents* (pp. 338–352). New York: Oxford University Press.

Greene, J. (2005b). Emotion and Cognition in Moral Judgment: Evidence from Neuroimaging. In J.-P. Changeux, A. Damasio, W. Singer, and Y. Christen (Eds.), *Neurobiology of Human Values* (pp. 57–66). Berlin/Heidelberg: Springer.

Greene, J. (2008). The Secret Joke of Kant's Soul. In W. Sinnott-Armstrong (Ed.), *Moral Psychology: Volume 3: The Neuroscience of Morality: Emotion, Brain Disorders, and Development* (pp. 35–80). Cambridge, MA: MIT Press.

Greene, J. (2009). Dual-process morality and the personal/impersonal distinction: A reply to McGuire, Langdon, Coltheart, and Mackenzie. *Journal of experimental Psychology, 45*(3), 581–584.

Greene, J. (2010). Notes on 'The Normative Insignificance of Neuroscience' by Selim Berker. Unpublished Manuscript, retrieved from <https://joshgreene.squarespace.com/s/notes-on-berker.pdf>.

Greene, J. (2013). *Moral Tribes: Emotion, Reason, and the Gap Between Us and Them*. New York: Penguin Press.

Greene, J. (2014). Beyond Point-and-Shoot Morality: Why Cognitive (Neuro)Science Matters for Ethics. *Ethics, 124*(4), 695–726.

Greene, J. (2016). Solving the Trolley Problem. In J. Sytsma and W. Buckwalter (Eds.), *A Companion to Experimental Philosophy* (pp. 175–189). Malden, MA: Wiley Blackwell.

Greene, J. (2017). The rat-a-gorical imperative: Moral intuition and the limits of affective learning. *Cognition, 167*(1), 66–77.

Greene, J., et al. (2001). An fMRI Investigation of Emotional Engagement in Moral Judgment. *Science, 293*(5537), 2105–2108.

Greene, J., et al. (2004). The Neural Bases of Cognitive Conflict and Control in Moral Judgment. *Neuron, 44*(2), 389–400.

Greene, J., et al. (2008). Cognitive load selectively interferes with utilitarian moral judgment. *Cognition, 107*(3), 1144–1154.

Greene, J., et al. (2009). Pushing Moral Buttons: The interaction between personal force and intention in moral judgment. *Cognition, 111*(3), 364–371.

Greene, J., and Young, L. (2020). The Cognitive Neuroscience of Moral Judgment and Decision-Making. In D. Poeppel, G. R. Mangun, and M. S. Gazzaniga (Eds.), *The Cognitive Neurosciences* (pp. 1003–1114). Cambridge, MA: MIT Press.

Greenspan, P. (2015). Confabulating the Truth: In Defense of 'Defensive' Moral Reasoning. *The Journal of Ethics, 19*(2), 105–123.

Grundmann, T. (2009). Reliabilism and the Problem of Defeaters. *Grazer Philosophische Studien, 79*(1), 65–76.

Grundmann, T. (2011). Defeasibility Theory. In S. Bernecker and D. Pritchard (Eds.), *The Routledge Companion to Epistemology* (pp. 156–166). Abingdon: Routledge.

Guthrie, S. (1993). *Faces in the Clouds: A New Theory of Religion*. New York/Oxford: Oxford University Press.

Hahn, U., and Oaksford, M. (2006). A Bayesian Approach to Informal Argument Fallacies. *Synthese, 152*(2), 207–236.

Haidt, J. (2001). The emotional dog and its rational tail: A social intuitionist approach to moral judgment. *Psychological Review, 108*(4), 814–834.

Haidt, J., et al. (2000). Moral dumbfounding: when intuition finds no reason. *Lund Psychological Reports, 1*(2), 1–23.

Hanson, L. (2017). The Real Problem with Evolutionary Debunking Arguments. *The Philosophical Quarterly, 67*(268), 508–533.

Harman, G. (1977). *The nature of morality: An introduction to ethics*. New York: Oxford University Press.

Hauser, M., et al. (2007). A Dissociation Between Moral Judgments and Justifications. *Mind and Language, 22*(1), 1–21.

Hawthorne, J. (2006). Three-Dimensionalism. In J. Hawthorne (Ed.), *Metaphysical Essays* (pp. 85 – 110). Oxford/New York: Oxford University Press.

Hayek, F. A. (1976). *Law, Legislation and Liberty: Volume 2. The Mirage of Social Justice.* Chicago: University of Chicago Press.

Hayek, F. A. (2006). *The Constitution of Liberty.* Abingdon: Routledge.

Heinzelmann, N. (2018). Deontology Defended. *Synthese, 195*(12):5197 – 5216.

Heller, M. (1990). *The ontology of physical objects: Four-dimensional hunks of matter.* Cambridge: Cambridge University Press.

Hinman, L. M. (1982). The case for *ad hominem* arguments. *Australasian Journal of Philosophy, 60*(4), 338 – 345.

Höffe, O. (2013). *Ethik: Eine Einführung.* München: C. H. Beck.

Hofmann, F. (2018). Evolution and Ethics: No Streetian Debunking of Moral Realism. *Croatian Journal of Philosophy, 18*(54), 399 – 414.

Hopster, J. (2018). Evolutionary arguments against moral realism: Why the empirical details matter (and which ones do). *Biology & Philosophy, 33*(5 – 6), 1 – 19.

Huemer, M. (2005). *Ethical Intuitionism.* Basingstoke/New York: Palgrave Macmillan.

Huemer, M. (2008). Revisionary Intuitionism. *Social Philosophy and Policy, 25*(1), 368 – 392.

Huemer, M. (2009). Singer's Unstable Meta-Ethics. In J. A. Schaler (Ed.), *Peter Singer Under Fire: The Moral Iconoclast Faces His Critics* (pp. 359 – 379). Chicago/La Salle: Open Court.

Huemer, M. (2013). *The Problem of Political Authority: An Examination of the Right to Coerce and the Duty to Obey.* Basingstoke: Palgrave Macmillan.

Jaquet, F. C. (2018). Evolution and Utilitarianism. *Ethical Theory and Moral Practice, 21*(5), 1151 – 1161.

Johnson, C. M. (2009). Reconsidering the *Ad Hominem. Philosophy, 84*(2), 251 – 266.

Joyce, R. (2001). *The Myth of Morality.* Cambridge: Cambridge University Press.

Joyce, R. (2005). Moral Fictionalism. In M. E. Kalderon (Ed.), *Fictionalism in Metaphysics* (pp. 287 – 313). Oxford/New York: Oxford University Press.

Joyce, R. (2006). *The Evolution of Morality.* Cambridge, MA: MIT Press.

Joyce, R. (2007). Morality, Schmorality. In P. Bloomfield (Ed.), *Morality and Self-Interest* (pp. 51 – 75). Oxford/New York: Oxford University Press.

Joyce, R. (2011). The Accidental Error Theorist. In R. Shafer-Landau (Ed.), *Oxford Studies in Metaethics: Volume 6* (pp. 153 – 180). Oxford/New York: Oxford University Press.

Joyce, R. (2013a). Ethics after Darwin. In M. Ruse (Ed.), *The Cambridge Encyclopedia of Darwin and Evolutionary Thought* (pp. 461 – 467). Cambridge: Cambridge University Press.

Joyce, R. (2013b). Ethics and Evolution. In H. LaFollette and I. Persson (Eds.), *The Blackwell Guide to Ethical Theory (2nd edition)* (pp. 123 – 147). Malden, MA: Blackwell.

Joyce, R. (2013c). The Evolutionary Debunking of Morality. In J. Feinberg and R. Shafer-Landau (Eds.), *Reason and Responsibility: Readings in Some Basic Problems of Philosophy (15th edition)* (pp. 527 – 534). Boston, MA: Cengage.

Joyce, R. (2013d). Irrealism and the Genealogy of Morals. *Ratio, 26*(4), 351 – 372.

Joyce, R. (2013e). The Many Moral Nativisms. In K. Sterelny, R. Joyce, B. Calcott, and B. J. Fraser (Eds.), *Cooperation and its Evolution* (pp. 549 – 572). Cambridge, MA: MIT Press.

Joyce, R. (2014). Taking Moral Skepticism Seriously. *Philosophical Studies, 168*(3), 843 – 851.

Joyce, R. (2016a). *Essays in Moral Skepticism.* Oxford: Oxford University Press.

Joyce, R. (2016b). Evolution and Moral Naturalism. In K. J. Clark (Ed.), *The Blackwell Companion to Naturalism* (pp. 369–385). Malden, MA: Blackwell.

Joyce, R. (2016c). Evolution, truth-tracking, and moral skepticism. In R. Joyce (Ed.), *Essays in Moral Skepticism* (pp. 142–158). Oxford: Oxford University Press.

Joyce, R. (2016d). Introduction: Morality: The Evolution of a Myth. In R. Joyce (Ed.), *Essays in Moral Skepticism* (pp. 1–16). Oxford: Oxford University Press.

Joyce, R. (2016e). Reply: Confessions of a Modest Debunker. In U. D. Leibowitz and N. Sinclair (Eds.), *Explanation in Ethics and Mathematics: Debunking and Dispensability* (pp. 124–148). Oxford: Oxford University Press.

Joyce, R. (2017). Human Morality: From an Empirical Puzzle to a Metaethical Puzzle. In M. Ruse and R. Richards (Eds.), *Cambridge Companion to Evolutionary Ethics* (pp. 101–113). Cambridge: Cambridge University Press.

Joyce, R. (2019). Moral Fictionalism: How to Have Your Cake and Eat It Too. In R. Garner (Ed.), *The End of Morality: Taking Abolitionism Seriously* (pp. 150–166). New York: Routledge.

Joyce, R. (2020). Fictionalism: Morality and Metaphor. In B. Armour-Garb and F. Kroon (Eds.), *Fictionalism in Philosophy* (pp. 103–121). New York: Oxford University Press.

Joyce, R., and Kirchin, S. (2010). Introduction. In R. Joyce and S. Kirchin (Eds.), *A World Without Values: Essays on John Mackie's Moral Error Theory* (pp. ix–xix). Dordrecht: Springer.

Kagan, S. (1989). *The Limits of Morality*. Oxford: Oxford University Press.

Kagan, S. (1998). *Normative Ethics*. Boulder, CO: Westview.

Kagan, S. (2016). Solving the Trolley Problem. In E. Rakowski (Ed.), *The Trolley Problem Mysteries* (pp. 151–168). New York: Oxford University Press.

Kahane, G. (2011). Evolutionary Debunking Arguments. *Noûs, 45*(1), 103–125.

Kahane, G. (2012). On the Wrong Track: Process and Content in Moral Psychology. *Mind and Language, 27*(5), 519–545.

Kahane, G. (2014a). Evolution and Impartiality. *Ethics, 124*(2), 327–341.

Kahane, G. (2014b). Intuitive and Counterintuitive Morality. In J. D'Arms and D. Jacobson (Eds.), *Moral Psychology and Human Agency: Philosophical Essays on the Science of Ethics* (pp. 9–39). Oxford: Oxford University Press.

Kahane, G. (2015). Sidetracked by trolleys: Why sacrificial moral dilemmas tell us little (or nothing) about utilitarian judgment. *Social Neuroscience, 10*(5), 551–560.

Kahane, G., et al. (2012). The neural basis of intuitive and counterintuitive moral judgment. *Social Cognitive and Affective Neuroscience, 7*(4), 393–402.

Kahane, G., et al. (2015). 'Utilitarian' judgments in sacrificial moral dilemmas do not reflect impartial concern for the greater good. *Cognition, 135*, 193–209.

Kahane, G., et al. (2018). Beyond Sacrificial Harm: A Two-Dimensional Model of Utilitarian Psychology. *Psychological Review, 125*(2), 131–164.

Kahane, G., and Shackel, N. (2010). Methodological Issues in the Neuroscience of Moral Judgment. *Mind and Language, 25*(5), 561–582.

Kahneman, D. (2003). A Perspective on Judgment and Choice: Mapping Bounded Rationality. *American Psychologist, 58*(9), 697–720.

Kamm, F. (1993). *Morality, Mortality: Volume 1*. New York: Oxford University Press.

Kamm, F. (2007). *Intricate Ethics: Rights, Responsibilities, and Permissible Harm*. Oxford: Oxford University Press.

Kauppinen, A. (2014). Ethics and Empirical Psychology – Critical Remarks ond Empirical Informed Ethics. In M. Christen, C. Van Schaik, J. Fischer, M. Huppenbauer, and C. Tanner (Eds.), *Empirically Informed Ethics: Morality Between Facts and Norms* (pp. 279–305). Cham: Springer.

Kelly, T. (2014). Evidence. In E. N. Zalta (Ed.), *The Stanford Encyclopedia of Philosophy*. Retrieved from <http://plato.stanford.edu/archives/fall2014/entries/evidence/>

Kershnar, S. (2000). A Defense of Retributivism. *International Journal of Applied Philosophy, 14*(1), 97–117.

Kitcher, P. (2011). *The Ethical Project*. Cambridge, MA: Harvard University Press.

Klein, C. (2011). The Dual Track Theory of Moral Decision-Making: a Critique of the Neuroimaging Evidence. *Neuroethics, 4*(2), 143–162.

Klenk, M. (2017). Old Wine in New Bottles: Evolutionary Debunking Arguments and the Benacerraf-Field Challenge. *Ethical Theory and Moral Practice, 20*(4), 781–795.

Klenk, M. (2020). Third Factor Explanations And Disagreement. *Synthese, 197*(1), 427–446.

Klenk, M. (forthcoming). Debunking, Epistemic Achievement, and Undermining Defeat. *American Philosophical Quarterly*.

Kohlberg, L. (1969). Stage and Sequence: The Cognitive-Developmental Approach to Socialization. In D. A. Goslin (Ed.), *Handbook of Socialization Theory and Research* (pp. 151–235). New York: Academic Press.

Korb, K. (2003). Bayesian Informal Logic and Fallacy. *Informal Logic, 23*(2), 41–70.

Korman, D. Z. (2014). Debunking Perceptual Beliefs about Ordinary Objects. *Philosophers' Imprint, 14*(13), 1–21.

Korman, D. Z. (2019). Debunking Arguments. *Philosophy Compass, 14*(12), 1–17.

Korsgaard, C. (1996). *The Sources of Normativity*. Cambridge: Cambridge Unitversity Press.

Kraaijeveld, S. R., and Sauer, H. (2019). Metamorality without Moral Truth. *Neuroethics, 12*(2), 119–131.

Kramer, M. H. (2009). *Moral Realism as a Moral Doctrine*. Malden, MA: Wiley-Blackwell.

Kumar, V., and Campbell, R. (2012). On the normative significance of experimental moral psychology. *Philosophical Psychology, 25*(3), 311–330.

Kumar, V., and May, J. (2019). How to Debunk Moral Beliefs. In J. Suikkannen and A. Kauppinen (Eds.), *Methodology and Moral Philosophy* (pp. 25–48). New York: Routledge.

Kurzban, R., et al. (2007). Audience effects on moralistic punishment. *Evolution and Human Behavior, 28*(2), 75–84.

Landy, J. F., and Goodwin, G. P. (2015). Does Incidental Disgust Amplify Moral Judgment? A Meta-Analytic Review of Experimental Evidence. *Perspectives on Psychological Science, 10*(4), 518–536.

Lasonen-Aarnio, M. (2014). Higher-Order Evidence and the Limits of Defeat. *Philosophy and Phenomenological Research, 88*(2), 314–345.

Leben, D. (2014). When psychology undermines beliefs. *Philosophical Psychology, 27*(3), 328–350.

Leibowitz, U. D., and Sinclair, N. (2017). Evolution and the Missing Link (in Debunking Arguments). In M. Ruse and R. J. Richards (Eds.), *The Cambridge Handbook of Evolutionary Ethics* (pp. 210–225). Cambridge: Cambridge University Press.

Leiter, B. (2004). The Hermeneutics of Suspicion: Recovering Marx, Nietzsche, and Freud. In B. Leiter (Ed.), *The Future of Philosophy* (pp. 74–105). Oxford: Clarendon Press.

Lenman, J. (2010). Humean Constructivism in Moral Theory. In R. Shafer-Landau (Ed.), *Oxford Studies in Metaethics: Volume 5* (pp. 175–194). Oxford: Oxford University Press.

Levy, N. (2006). Cognitive Scientific Challenges to Morality. *Philosophical Psychology, 19*(5), 567–587.

Liao, M. S., et al. (2012). Putting the Trolley in Order: Experimental Philosophy and the Loop Case. *Philosophical Psychology, 25*(5), 661–671.

Lieberman, D., et al. (2003). Does morality have a biological basis? An empirical test of the factors governing moral sentiments relating to incest. *Proceedings of the Royal Society London, B*(270), 819–826.

Lott, M. (2016). Moral Implications from Cognitive (Neuro)Science? No Clear Route. *Ethics, 127*(1), 241–256.

Lumer, C. (1990). *Praktische Argumentationstheorie: Theoretische Grundlagen, praktische Begründung und Regeln wichtiger Argumentationsarten.* Braunschweig/Wiesbaden: Vieweg.

Lumer, C. (2005). The Epistemological Theory of Argument – How and Why? *Informal Logic, 25*(3), 213–243.

Lutz, M. (2018). What Makes Evolution a Defeater? *Erkenntnis, 83*(6), 1105–1126.

Machery, E., and Mallon, R. (2010). Evolution of Morality. In J. M. Doris and the Moral Psychology Research Group (Eds.), *The Moral Psychology Handbook* (pp. 3–46). Oxford, New York: Oxford University Press.

Mackie, J. L. (1977). *Ethics: Inventing Right and Wrong.* Harmondsworth, New York: Penguin.

Marx, K., and Engels, F. (2012). *The Communist Manifesto.* London/New York: Verso.

Mason, K. (2010). Debunking Arguments and the Genealogy of Religion and Morality. *Philosophy Compass, 5*(9), 770–778.

Mason, K. (2011). Moral Psychology and Moral Intuitions: A Pox On All Your Houses. *Australasian Journal of Philosophy, 89*(3), 441–458.

May, J. (2018). *Regard for Reason in the Moral Mind.* Oxford: Oxford University Press.

McGuire, J., et al. (2009). A reanalysis of the peronsal/impersonal distinction in moral psychology research. *Journal of Experimental Social Psychology, 45*(3), 577–580.

McIntyre, A. (2014). Doctrine of Double Effect. In E. N. Zalta (Ed.), *The Stanford Encyclopedia of Philosophy.* Retrieved from <https://plato.stanford.edu/archives/win2014/entries/double-effect/>

McMahan, J. (2013). Moral Intuition. In H. LaFollette and I. Persson (Eds.), *The Blackwell Guide to Ethical Theory (2nd Edition)* (pp. 103–120). Malden, MA: Blackwell.

McNaughton, D., and Rawling, P. (2003). Descriptivism, Normativity, and the Metaphysics of Reasons. *Proceedings of the Aristotelian Society, Supplementary Volumes, 77*(1), 23–45.

Mihailov, E. (2016). Is Deontology a Moral Confabulation? *Neuroethics, 9*(1), 1–13.

Morton, J. (2016). A New Evolutionary Debunking Argument Against Moral Realism. *Journal of the American Philosophical Association, 2*(2), 233–253.

Morton, J. (2018a). A Dilemma for Streetian Constructivism. *Southwest Philosophy Review, 34*(1), 133–140.

Morton, J. (2018b). When Do Replies to the Evolutionary Debunking Argument Against Moral Realism Beg the Question? *Australasian Journal of Philosophy, 97*(2), 265–280.

Musen, J. D., and Greene, J. (MS). Mere Spatial Distance Weakens Perceived Moral Obligation to Help Those in Desperate Need. Unpublished Manuscript.

Nagel, T. (1970). *The Possibility of Altruism.* Oxford: Oxford University Press.

Nichols, S. (2014). Process Debunking and Ethics. *Ethics, 124*(4), 727–749.

Nietzsche, F. (1996). *On the Genealogy of Morals*. Oxford/New York: Oxford University Press.

Nisbett, R. E., and Wilson, T. D. (1977). Telling More Than We Know: Verbal Reports on Mental Processes. *Psychological Review, 84*(3), 231–259.

Nozick, R. (1981). *Philosophical Explanations*. Cambridge, MA: Harvard University Press.

Nozick, R. (1997). Why Do Intellectuals Oppose Capitalism? In R. Nozick (Ed.), *Socratic Puzzles* (pp. 280–295). Cambridge, MA: Harvard University Press.

Nye, H. (2015). Directly Plausible Principles. In C. Daly (Ed.), *The Palgrave Handbook of Philosphical Methods*. New York: Palgrave Macmillan.

Olson, J. (2009). Reasons and the New Naturalism. In S. Robertson (Ed.), *Spheres of Reason: New Essays in the Philosophy of Normativity* (pp. 164–182). Oxford/New York: Oxford University Press.

Parfit, D. (1993). Reasons and Motivation. *Proceedings of the Aristotelian Society, 71*(1), 99–130.

Parfit, D. (2011a). *On What Matters: Volume 1*. Oxford: Oxford University Press.

Parfit, D. (2011b). *On What Matters: Volume 2*. Oxford: Oxford University Press.

Paulo, N. (2019). In Search of Greene's Argument. *Utilitas, 31*(1), 38–58.

Paxton, J. M., et al. (2014). Are 'counter-intuitive' deontological judgments really counter-intuitive? An empirical reply to Kahane et al. (2012). *Social Cognitive and Affective Neuroscience, 9*(9), 1368–1371.

Persson, I., and Savulescu, J. (2012). *Unfit for the Future*. Oxford: Oxford University Press.

Petrinovich, L., and O'Neill, P. (1996). Influence of Wording and Framing Effects on Moral Intuitions. *Ethology and Sociobiology, 17*(3), 145–171.

Piaget, J. (1997). *Moral Judgment and the Child*. New York: Free Press Paperbacks.

Plantinga, A. (1993). *Warrant and Proper Function*. New York: Oxford University Press.

Plato. (1979). *Gorgias (transl. with notes by T. Irwin)*. Oxford: Clarendon Press.

Plato. (2012). *The Republic (transl. by C. Rowe)*. New York: Penguin.

Pollock, J. L. (1986). *Contemporary Theories of Knowledge*. Totowa, NJ: Rowman and Littlefield.

Prinz, J. (2007). *The Emotional Construction of Morals*. Oxford/New York: Oxford University Press.

Putnam, D. (2010). Equivocating the *Ad Hominem*. *Philosophy, 85*(4), 551–555.

Quinn, W. (1993). Actions, Intentions, and Consequences: The Doctrine of Double Effect. In W. Quinn (Ed.), *Morality and Action* (pp. 175–193). Cambridge: Cambridge University Press.

Railton, P. (1986). Facts and Values. *Philosophical Topics, 14*(2), 5–31.

Railton, P. (2014). The Affective Dog and Its Rational Tale: Intuition and Attunement. *Ethics, 124*(4), 813–859.

Reichenbach, H. (1938). *Experience and Prediction: An Analysis of the Foundations and the Structure of Knowledge*. Chicago/London: The University of Chicago Press.

Rini, R. A. (2013). Making Psychology Normatively Significant. *The Journal of Ethics, 17*(3), 257–274.

Rini, R. A. (2016). Debunking debunking: a regress challenge for psychological threats to moral judgment. *Philosophical Studies, 173*(3), 675–697.

Risberg, O., and Tersman, F. (2020). Moral Realism and the Argument from Skepticism. *International Journal for the Study of Skepticism, 10*(3–4), 283–303.

Rodogno, R. (2016). Prudential value or well-being. In T. Brosch and D. Sander (Eds.), *Oxford Handbook of Value: The Affective Sciences of Values and Valuation* (pp. 287–312). Oxford: Oxford University Press.

Rosati, C. (1996). Internalism and the Good for a Person. *Ethics, 106*(2), 297–326.

Rowland, R. (2019). Local Evolutionary Debunking Arguments. *Philosophical Perspectives, 33*(1), 170–199.

Ruse, M. (1986). *Taking Darwin Seriously*. Oxford: Basil Blackwell.

Ruse, M. (2006). Is Darwinian Metaethics Possible (And If It Is, Is It Well Taken)? In G. Boniolo and G. De Anna (Eds.), *Evolutionary Ethics and Contemporary Biology* (pp. 13–26). Cambridge: Cambridge University Press.

Ruse, M., and Wilson, E. O. (1985). The evolution of ethics. *The New Scientist, 108*(1478), 50–52.

Sandberg, J., and Juth, N. (2011). Ethics and Intuitions: A Reply to Singer. *Journal of Ethics, 15*(3), 209–226.

Sauer, H. (2012a). Educated Intuitions: Automaticity and Rationality in Moral Judgment. *Philosophical Explorations, 15*(3), 255–275.

Sauer, H. (2012b). Morally irrelevant factors: What's left of the dual process-model of moral cognition? *Philosophical Psychology, 25*(6), 783–811.

Sauer, H. (2018). *Debunking Arguments in Ethics*. Cambridge: Cambridge University Press.

Schafer, K. (2010). Evolution and Normative Scepticism. *Australasian Journal of Philosophy, 88*(3), 471–488.

Schnall, S., et al. (2008). Disgust as Embodied Moral Judgment. *Personality and Social Psychology Bulletin, 34*(8), 1096–1109.

Schoenfield, M. (2014). A Dilemma for Calibrationism. *Philosophy and Phenomenological Research, 91*(2), 425–455.

Schwitzgebel, E., and Cushman, F. (2012). Expertise in Moral Reasoning? Order Effects on Moral Judgment in Professional Philosophers and Non-Philosophers. *Mind & Language, 27*(2), 135–153.

Schwitzgebel, E., and Cushman, F. (2015). Philosophers' biased judgments persist despite training, expertise and reflection. *Cognition, 141*, 127–137.

Schwitzgebel, E., and Ellis, J. (2017). Rationalization in Moral and Philosophical Thought. In J.-F. Bonnefon and B. Trémolière (Eds.), *Moral Inferences* (pp. 170–190). Hove: Psychology Press.

Searle, J. R. (1993). Rationality and Reason, What is at Stake? *Daedalus, 122*(4), 55–83.

Shafer-Landau, R. (2003). *Moral Realism: A Defence*. New York: Oxford University Press.

Shafer-Landau, R. (2012). Evolutionary Debunking, Moral Realism, and Moral Knowledge. *Journal of Ethics and Social Philosophy, 7*(1), 1–37.

Shenhav, A., and Greene, J. (2014). Integrative Moral Judgment: Dissociating the Roles of the Amygdala and Ventromedial Prefrontal Cortex. *The Journal of Neuroscience, 34*(14), 4741–4749.

Sider, T. (2001). *Four-Dimensionalism: An Ontology of Persistence and Time*. Oxford/New York: Oxford University Press.

Sidgwick, H. (1981). *The Methods of Ethics*. Indianapolis: Hackett Publishing.

Siegel, H., and Biro, J. (1997). Epistemic Normativity, Argumentation, and Fallacies. *Argumentation, 11*(3), 277–292.

Singer, P. (1972). Famine, Affluence, and Morality. *Philosophy and Public Affairs, 1*(3), 229 – 243.

Singer, P. (1993). *Practical Ethics.* Cambridge: Cambridge University Press.

Singer, P. (1999). A Response. In D. Jamieson (Ed.), *Singer and his Critics* (pp. 269 – 335). Malden, MA: Blackwell.

Singer, P. (2005). Ethics and Intuitions. *The Journal of Ethics, 9*(3 – 4), 331 – 352.

Singer, P., and de Lazari-Radek, K. (2016). Doing our best for hedonistic utilitarianism: Reply to our critics. *Etica & Politica, 18*(1), 187 – 207.

Skarsaune, K. O. (2011). Darwin and moral realism: survival of the iffiest. *Philosophical Studies, 152*(2), 229 – 243.

Smith, M. (1994). *The Moral Problem.* Malden, MA: Blackwell.

Sober, E., and Wilson, D. S. (1999). *Unto Others: The Evolution and Psychology of Unselfish Behaviour.* Cambridge, MA: Harvard University Press.

Sosa, E. (1999). How to Defeat Opposition to Moore. *Philosophical Perspectives, 33*(13), 141 – 153.

Sperber, D. (1996). *Explaining Culture: A Naturalistic Approach.* Oxford: Blackwell.

Srinivasan, A. (2015). The Archimedean Urge. *Philosophical Perspectives, 29*(1), 325 – 362.

Street, S. (2006). A Darwinian Dilemma for Realist Theories of Value. *Philosophical Studies, 127*(1), 109 – 166.

Street, S. (2008a). Constructivism About Reasons. In R. Shafer-Landau (Ed.), *Oxford Studies in Metaethics: Volume 3* (pp. 208 – 245). Oxford/New York: Oxford University Press.

Street, S. (2008b). Reply to Copp: Naturalism, Normativity, and the Varieties of Realism Worth Worrying About. *Philosophical Issues, 18*(1), 207 – 228.

Street, S. (2009). In Defense of Future Tuesday Indifference. *Philosophical Issues, 19*(1), 273 – 298.

Street, S. (2010). What is Constructivism in Ethics and Metaethics? *Philosophy Compass, 5*(5), 363 – 384.

Street, S. (2012). Coming to Terms With Contingency: Humean Constructivism About Reasons. In J. Lenman and Y. Shemmer (Eds.), *Constructivism in Practical Philosophy* (pp. 40 – 59). Oxford: Oxford University Press.

Street, S. (2015). Does Anything Really Matter or Did We Just Evolve to Think So? In G. Rosen, A. Byrne, J. Cohen, and S. Shiffrin (Eds.), *The Norton Introduction to Philosophy* (pp. 685 – 692). New York: Norton.

Street, S. (2016). Objectivity and Truth: You'd Better Rethink It. In R. Shafer-Landau (Ed.), *Oxford Studies in Metaethics: Volume 11* (pp. 293 – 333). New York: Oxford University Press.

Streumer, B. (2017). *Unbelievable Errors: An Error Theory About All Normative Judgments.* Oxford: Oxford University Press.

Sunstein, C. R. (2005). Moral Heuristics. *Behavioral and Brain Sciences, 28*(4), 531 – 542.

Tersman, F. (2008). The reliability of moral intuitions: A challenge from neuroscience. *Australasian Journal of Philosophy, 86*(3), 389 – 405.

Tersman, F. (2019). From Scepticism to Anti-Realism. *dialectica, 73*(3), 411 – 427.

Thomson, J. J. (1976). Killing, Letting Die, and the Trolley Problem. *The Monist, 59*(2), 204 – 217.

Thurow, J. C. (2013). Does cognitive science show belief in god to be irrational? The epistemic consquences of the cognitive science of religion. *International Journal for Philosophy of Religion, 74*(1), 77 – 98.

Timmons, M. (2008). Toward a Sentimentalist Deontology. In W. Sinnott-Armstrong (Ed.), *Moral Psychology* (pp. 93–104). Cambridge, MA: MIT Press.

Tisak, M. S., and Turiel, E. (1984). Children's Conceptions of Moral and Prudential Rules. *Child Development, 55*(3), 1030–1039.

Tobia, K. (2015). Moral Tribes: Emotion, Reason, and the Gap between Us and Them. *Philosophical Psychology, 28*(5), 746–750.

Tobia, K., et al. (2013a). Moral Intuitions: Are Philosophers Experts? *Philosophical Psychology, 26*(5), 629–638.

Tobia, K., et al. (2013b). Cleanliness is Next to Morality, Even for Philosophers. *Journal of Consciousness Studies, 20*(11–12), 195–205.

Tropman, E. (2013). Evolutionary debunking arguments: moral realism, constructivism, and explaining moral knowledge. *Philosophical Explorations, 17*(2), 126–140.

Uhlmann, E. L., et al. (2009). The motivated use of moral principles. *Judgment and Decision Making, 4*(6), 476–491.

Unger, P. (1997). *Living High and Letting Die: Our Illusion of Innocence.* New York: Oxford University Press.

Vavova, K. (2014). Debunking evolutionary debunking. In R. Shafer-Landau (Ed.), *Oxford Studies in Metaethics: Volume 9* (pp. 76–101). Oxford: Oxford University Press.

Vavova, K. (2018). Irrelevant Influences. *Philosophy and Phenomenological Research, 96*(1), 134–152.

von Mises, L. (1972). *The Anticapitalistic Mentality.* Grove City, PA: Libertarian Press.

Wedgewood, R. (2011). Defending Double Effect. *Ratio, 24*(4), 384–401.

Weinberg, J. M., et al. (2010). Are philosophers expert intuiters. *Philosophical Psychology, 23*(3), 331–355.

Wheatley, T., and Haidt, J. (2005). Hypnotic Disgust Makes Moral Judgments More Severe. *Psychological Science, 16*(10), 780–784.

White, R. (2010). You Just Believe That Because… *Philosophical Perspectives, 24*(1), 573–615.

Wiech, K., et al. (2013). Cold or calculating? Reduced activity in the subgenual cingulate cortex reflects decreased emotional aversion to harming in counterintuitive utilitarian judgment. *Cognition, 126*(3), 364–372.

Wiegmann, A., et al. (2012). Order effects in moral judgment. *Philosophical Psychology, 25*(6), 813–836.

Wiegmann, A., et al. (2020). Intuitive Expertise and Irrelevant Options. In T. Lombrozo, J. Knobe, and S. Nichols (Eds.), *Oxford Studies in Experimental Philosophy: Volume 3* (pp. 275–310). Oxford: Oxford University Press.

Wielenberg, E. J. (2010). On the Evolutionary Debunking of Morality. *Ethics, 120*(3), 441–464.

Wielenberg, E. J. (2014). Joshua Greene: Moral Tribes: Emotion, Reason, and the Gap between Us and Them. *Ethics, 124*(4), 910–916.

Wilson, D. S. (2002). *Darwin's Cathedral: Evolution, Religion, and the Nature of Society.* Chicago: University of Chicago Press.

Wilson, T. D. (2002). *Strangers to ourselves: Discovering the adaptive unconscious.* Cambridge, MA: Harvard University Press.

Wilson, T. D., and Nisbett, R. E. (1978). The Accuracy of Verbal Reports About the Effects of Stimuli on Evaluations and Behavior. *Social Psychology, 41*(2), 118–131.

Index

www.ingramcontent.com/pod-product-compliance
Lightning Source LLC
Chambersburg PA
CBHW022134080426
42734CB00006B/362